His Presence

By
Carolyn Ruth Washington

... The upright shall dwell in your presence (before your face) Psalm 140:13

Carolyn Ruth Washington

Dedications

This book is dedicated to all that played a role in the adversities of my life. For it was but for the Grace of God that I've learned from my adversities that brought me into the full knowledge of the greatest love of all: Jesus Christ, God's Son and the importance of His presence in my life.

Also, I wish to express my appreciation to my parents, Reverend George and Abbie Washington, who await me in glory, my two siblings, Gwendolyn and Marilyn, their beautiful children and grandchildren ...my wonderful nieces and nephews ... for sharing my life on earth. We will be sharing eternity together because our parents taught us about God's love and the riches we have through Jesus Christ. Both my parents and my siblings taught me what it truly means to trust in God with your whole heart. This was accomplished through their demonstration of His love and through my witness of His presence in their lives.

To all my loving relatives and friends both natural and spiritual and a special recognition to my lovely daughter, Iris Ruth, whom God gave to me and whom I gave my middle name. The name "Ruth" means "special friend" also "stay put". You really have been a 'Spirit of Ruth' in my life. May God grant you your Kinsman redeemer in the person of God's choice. Iris Ruth you have been faithful.

Thanks to Nancy, Ernestine and Rob for their dedication and patience. Gratitude and honor to Juanita Darling, my Peach, who taught me the essence of a godly woman by her example and by her servitude. To all that shared my life rather good or bad, you led me to His presence where He promises to never leave me nor forsake me. And most of all to my precious Lord, Redeemer and Lover of my soul, it is my pleasure to share how your presence guides, teaches, leads, comforts and abides with us always. This book is dedicated to you and what it means to me to please you my King.

Table of Contents

Foreword

W hen I said this would be a difficult task, I meant that in every sense of the word. Starting a new career after all those years of pondering with the idea, not knowing how to get started, not to mention the possibility of failure, which in and of itself, is difficult. But here lies the truth of my urgency to complete what was birthed in me and that is to write.

I've always known I wanted to be a writer. I've written countless poems, words of expressions, divine thoughts. They often are my solace and I just love playing with words and seeing them in print. It wasn't until now that I've received a prophetic word that I should write. That's when I stopped pondering and started believing that it's possible.

Well, this is the beginning of beginnings and to tell you the truth, I have so much within me I must write about it.

But I will begin with 'His Presence' because without Him I'm nothing. I began this book in the year 2008, which is the year 5768 in the Hebraic calendar. The number eight always links to new beginnings and that is when I started. In the year 2009, 5769 in the Hebraic calendar, the number nine always has significance with new birthing, births of things conceived. The conception of 'His Presence' began.

I remember that as early as elementary school, I desired God's presence in my life. I recall my mother coming to the Pentecostal church in Perrine, Florida and getting me off my knees as I was seeking the Lord. It would be as late as midnight on a school night. My voice would be hoarse, I would be tired and still feeling empty. All I wanted was to feel His presence so very badly. But on weekends, I was allowed to stay as long as the church doors were opened. This went on for many years.

Not realizing God has always been there with me, I spent many years seeking His presence. What a joy it is when you know that He is always with you. That's when you learn to rejoice. Like the apostle Paul says, *"Rejoice in the Lord always, Again I will say rejoice."* He will never leave you in your mess, nor will He forsake you and He will always allow you a way of escape out of your mess. Speaking of mess, what a mess I was without my realizing the truth of His presence in my life.

Preface

Divine revelation has revealed to me why I am compelled to write. I know this will be a difficult task but I do know one thing; God is with me. I have no doubt of His presence in my life. I know He will not leave me nor forsake me, and this book is a revelation of this fact. I have come to know God for myself. His presence is all that I seek and my relationship with Him will appear clear and evident in the reading of this book. God's supernatural interventions into the many tests and trials mentioned are the visible signs that God desires a personal relationship with me, with all of us. His presence is all we should be seeking.

Sometimes it takes a life time for us to realize the significance of His presence in our lives. It has been difficult for me to share my personal experiences which most individuals would never voice, let alone publish for all to see.

For years I battled with depression, obesity and all kinds of illnesses, hospitalizations, including a mental institution and countless failed relationships, to finally be able to embrace the significance of His presence in my life. To tell you the truth, I almost died before the essence of His presence became important to me, but now that I know its importance, I will guard it with my life.

I want to share with you so that you can know this precious promise in its fullness. God promised over and over in His word that He will never leave you nor forsake you. When Joshua took over the mantle of leading the children of Israel across the Jordan, God told him: *"just like I was with Moses so I will be with you." (Joshua 1:5)* Let me emphasize, just like He has been in my life, He too will be in your life. Just look around you, you will recognize His presence has been there all along, for you. Embrace Him before you don't have the opportunity to. I almost didn't.

Thank God I did!

The importance of writing this book is to let the world know His presence is all that we should be seeking in life. For where His presence is there is fullness, life abundant. Once you embrace His presence, nothing in life matters except to remain there. For so long, we have sought after everything and still we are not satisfied. Material things, mates, children, friendships, power or whatever, nothing really satisfies us. That is why God said: *"But seek first the kingdom of God and His righteousness, and all these things shall be added to you.' (Matt. 6:33).* Not until we return to basics, seeking after Him and obeying Him, can we sense His presence in its fullness and our land will not be desolate like our lives.

Jeremiah 9: 12-13 says: *"What man is wise enough to understand this? Who has been instructed by the Lord and can explain it? Why has the land been ruined and laid waste like a desert that no one can cross? The Lord said, "It is because they have forsaken my law, which I set before them; they have not obeyed me or followed my law."*

We can never be satisfied until we acknowledge God's presence and seek to obey Him. I had to learn that the hard way. By refusing to acknowledge Him and continuing to go from one sin to another left me in a state of desolation, thus having to be refined and tested in a furnace of afflictions.

I learned the hard truth that the afflictions of the righteous are many, but God delivers us right out of them all. I now abide in Him and Him alone. My trust is in the one who delivers. Psalms 119: 50 says: *"This is my comfort in my affliction for thy word hath quickened me."* God's word is what makes us come alive to His truth, and He is the way to the truth and life. I'm hiding in Him for He is my refuge. *"Trust in Him at all time, ye people, pour out your heart before Him. God is a refuge for us." (Psalms 62:8)*

This all began for me when I poured out my heart before the Lord at a crossroad in my life. I chose to start a "fast" asking for direction on what to do. Well, this fast lasted for thirty days and resulted in a trip to jail, a trip to the mental hospital and 23 years of trying to figure out exactly what God had shown me during that time. Everything happened as a result of this fast without food or water. Later on I will go into more details, but for now let me give you a brief synopsis.

In 1986, in Raleigh, North Carolina, I started to live an open vision that lasted several months. This vision started when I began an extended FAST. I heard the trumpet sound, I was called up into heaven, and I witnessed my life on trial at the judgment seat of believers. I can clearly remember thinking how real everything was. I also returned from heaven to reign and to live with Christ in the 'New Earth'. The peace I experienced during this time can only be explained as a total state of rest like nothing you could ever imagine. I also remember having three distinctive births in this vision. On October 19, 2008, as I was preaching at Homestead Correctional Institution, I was given a spiritual birth to the revelations I had been carrying within me for twenty years. This launched me into prophetic ministry and it was only when I started to write this book that the significance of the births began to unfold.

I received the following verse: Philippians 4:4, *"Rejoice in the Lord always, Again I will say rejoice"*. To God be all the glory, He has instructed me to tell His people to rejoice. This is a command. He does not want us to faint in the day of adversity, nor does He want us to let our strength be small, for He is coming soon.

In addition I also experienced the rapture, the judgment seat and the reign of our Lord and Savior, Jesus Christ, on earth. It is with urgency that I write this book in hopes to help motivate and prepare His bride, the church, for the rapture. He wants us to know that the rapture is the reward for His faithful. *"His lord said to him; Well done, good and faithful servant; you have been faithful over a few things, I will make you ruler over many things. Enter into the joy of your lord."* *(Matt.25:23)*

For two years after I experienced the vision, God kept me in silence so that I would not speak of it in unbelief.

Like Habakkuk, *'though the vision tarries, wait.'* I waited as my life unfolded. Like Joshua in Jericho, God instructed the Israelites to do three things: wait, walk and keep their mouth shut until it was time to shout. I waited like Habakkuk, I walked it out like Joshua in Jericho and I remained silent until instructed.

Jericho was to be the Israelites first conquest of victory after crossing over into their promised land. It was to be taken as a blueprint for future victories, their first fruit offering of obedience to God. I trust this book is my beginning of beginnings, my first fruit offering in trusting Him with all He has entrusted to me, so that I may share with you, the reader.

His Presence

Guides Us

I now truly identify with David when he asked the Lord in the Psalms, not to take His presence from him. *"Do not cast me from your presence or take your Holy Spirit from me." (Psalm51:11)*

After all these years of messing up; Lord, please don't withdraw your Spirit from me. For you see, you will never know the importance of His presence until you allow Him to reveal himself to you. And when He withdraws Himself from you, He often is teaching you He is jealous, for 'Jealous' is His covenant name for His people. *"For thou shalt worship no other god: for the Lord, whose name is Jealous, is a jealous God." (Exodus 34:14)* The first four of the Ten Commandments given to Moses to give to His chosen people make specific note of His desire to be one with them.

"I am the Lord thy God, which brought thee out of the land of Egypt, from the house of bondage. Thou shalt have none other gods before me."

Thou shalt not make thee any graven image, or any likeness of anything that is in heaven above, or that is in the waters beneath the earth."

"Thou shalt not bow down thyself unto them, nor serve them: for I the Lord thy God am a jealous God, visiting the iniquity of the fathers upon the children unto the third and fourth generation of them that hate me."

"But showing mercy to thousands of those who love me and keep my commands." (Deuteronomy 5: 6-10)

God wants an intimate personal relationship with each one of us. He wants to make covenant with us. Early on in my childhood, I wanted the Lord to have an active role in my life. I had accepted Him as my Lord and grew up having Him with me. However, like David I did my dirt. My spiritual Mom, Lovie Debnam, in North Carolina once said to me "Carolyn you are just like David, you do your dirt and run back to the Lord." She had about 10 natural children and just as many spiritual children. Thank God for His presence even when we do not realize it. I now know that God had specifically placed Ma Debnam in my early adult life for spiritual guidance.

I'll try not to get ahead of myself. I grew up attending church. My father was a pastor with a third grade education. And because he could not read very well, I would help him with his sermons, with word pronunciations, meanings and sometimes, I even gave him input on what I thought the passage meant. Here I was an elementary school age child writing sermons. And just like David appeared to be prematurely promoted in the eyes of the world to fight Goliath, I also had been prematurely promoted to prepare sermons. "Saul replied...*you are only a boy*... then he said to David... *Go, and the Lord be with you!*" *(I Samuel 17:33-37)*

David had learned to trust the Lord who had helped him with many adversaries and obstacles like the lion, the bear, and other annoying oppositions that came his way. We should never fear opposition. Instead, we are to run to God, repent if we caused the opposition, and be watchful. But most assuredly we need to stand firm and not faint just because it seems stronger than our self. God uses what you entrust to him and gives you the boldness needed to cause you to triumph with confidence of His guidance.

When I think about the years of stumbling and falling, not to mention getting back up again, I still did not understand the true essence of God's presence. It wasn't until God allowed me to be broken, did I then realize what David meant. *"The sacrifices of God are a broken spirit; a broken and contrite heart, O God, you will not despise."* Psalms 51:17 tells us we can't offer up our messes as just any sacrifice, only our pure hearts.

So many times we look around and we find ourselves completely separated from Him because of our own selfish desires. And, like David in Psalms 51, when he was confronted with his selfish act, he realized that God's presence could be withdrawn. O, God don't take your spirit from me he cried.

Many of us today have this same cry. Because of our selfish desires, like abortions, we too cry; *"Deliver me from the guilt of bloodshed, O God, you who are God my Savior, and my tongue will sing of your righteousness." (Psalms 51:14)*

I personally know that many of us have used abortions as birth control, having one abortion after another, and the results are guilt and shame. O' God save us, renew in us a clean heart. Restoration will come when we do what David declared he would do if God restored him. *"Then I will teach transgressors your ways, and sinners will turn back to you."*

While teaching Sunday school at a missionary Baptist church one Sunday morning, the Lord led me to give my testimony about having an abortion, and how God guided me through this very difficult struggle. At this time, I was advised by doctors to have an abortion because I had a history of blood clots that had gone into my lungs on two different occasions. I was informed that I would have to be on bed rest and be given injections daily. And, if there were complications, they might have to make the difficult decision to save one of us, the child or me.

So I made the decision to abort the baby. But that didn't solve the problems, it created new ones. I had to live with elongated years of regret and guilt because of this abortion, as well as the lack of trust I had in God to keep the baby. But with that said, God had given me a powerful testimony for that Sunday.

I received a knock at my door from a student in my Sunday school class. I met her outside the door and as she stood there glowing, pretty as a peach, I immediately commented how her radiance was that of a pregnant woman. She had come to ask me for money but not to tell me what it was for. When I asked her if she was pregnant, she broke down and told me she wanted to have an abortion. I began to share with her my regrets, my shame and my guilt. I gave her detailed testimony and told her the truth, that abortion is not just the end of a pregnancy; it will be something you will live with the rest of your life. Every time you hear a baby cry, or you see a child that would be the age of your aborted child, you will be reminded. I am happy to say she made the decision to keep the baby and I have a handsome God Son that loves the Lord and has made a vow to do whatever God calls him to do in his life. His mother would always remind me "you are going to help me with him, you advised me to have him", especially when he would get himself in trouble as boys often do. And she continued to remind me even as he got ready to go to college.

Unless you are willing to be transparent in your struggles, others can't see how God works in them. Our testimonies can be fruitful for both people involved. I have always said that God has given me a fruit that remains. Even though I don't have any natural children of my own, He continues to use the difficult times in my life and gives me beauty for my ashes. Let me say here, just be willing to be obedient when He asks you to share your testimony. Be willing like David to be restored and ask God for guidance and His mercy.

"Have mercy on me, O God, according to your unfailing love; according to your great compassion. Wash away all my iniquity and cleanse me from my sin. For I know my transgressions, and my sin is always before me. Against you, you only, have I sinned and done what is evil in your sight, so that you are proved right when you speak and justified when you judge. Surely I was sinful at birth, sinful from the time my mother conceived me. Surely you desire truth in the inner parts; you teach me wisdom in the inmost place..." (Psalms 51:1-6)

It is in the innermost places where God tests and examines us, the very center of our emotions and moral sensitivity. Our creator knows His creation. He searches the places man can't see, because He knows His creation; even our stumbling and falling and our getting up. He cares for all of us, especially our souls. *"Now may the God of peace Himself sanctify you completely; and may your whole spirit, soul, and body be preserved blameless at the coming of our Lord Jesus Christ." (1 Thessalonians 5:23)*

There is nothing that is not privy to Him, even in our mother's womb. Not only that, God has ordained all our days before we began one of them; according to Psalms 139:1-18. There is no escaping His presence. We are to submit our whole spirit, soul and body completely to God, for He is worthy and we are called into His glorious kingdom. The Holy Spirit will help us work out the sanctifying process.

All this time I was just going through the motions, of trying to be a good Christian not realizing that God had me already hemmed in. He goes before us and behind us. *"Surely goodness and mercy shall follow us." (Psalm 23:6)* Even when we fail miserably, His mighty hand is upon His creation. Years later after the abortion, in order to have another child, I conceived again out of wedlock. I had convinced myself that God knew my heart and how much it would mean to me to have this child. But after listening to the advice of my spiritual mom, Ma Debnam, I openly repented before the church and I followed through in obedience. I went before my church and asked for their forgiveness for intentionally getting pregnant out of wedlock.

I felt in my heart I could do this. As crazy as this sounds, I felt that if I had this child and did not abort it, God would forgive me for not trusting Him the first time. To tell you the truth, I had fear and doubt all along. And these fears and doubts manifested into the biggest heartache of my life. After going through all that humiliation of standing before the church and asking for forgiveness, I was only able to carry the child for five months and I had a miscarriage.

I was teaching junior high school at the time, and to have a single teacher pregnant out of wedlock was a big 'no no' in the rural area of Garner, North Carolina. So I took a leave of absence at the end of the school year. That summer I was working at a church day care which was in its start-up phase. I was hired as the Director. I did all of this so I could have this baby I so desperately thought I needed to fill the void of the abortion.

The day care opened that fall and early one morning as I was arriving, my water broke. After being rushed to the hospital and hours of waiting for the baby to come on its own, the doctors finally decided to induce labor. I lost a little baby girl at five months. Back then technology was not of such to save her, but now it is possible.

Many years later I was reading an article in the Baptist Hospital Resource Magazine where a five month old fetus survived. Again I felt like David did after losing his child with Bathsheba. I cried out for mercy and forgiveness, asking God to search my heart and renew a right spirit within me.

While I was in the hospital recovering from the miscarriage, I needed to go into surgery for a DNC. This was followed with a severe case of depression. Oh how I cried and I cried. Now I know not to put God to any foolish test. That's exactly what I did when I thought I could have a baby out of wedlock. It was foolish of me to think I could gain God's approval after aborting my first child. What utter nonsense. Like David was grieving over the sickness of his child that eventually died, so was I. God will not be mocked. What you sow you will also reap. And if you sow to your flesh, you will reap corruption. However, if you sow to the spirit you will reap eternal life.

There is always a consequence for our actions. Even David's actions resulted in a consequence, and God used Nathan to rebuke David. (2 Samuel 12:11-24) When you read the details of the death of David's child, you will learn that after the child died David rose up and worshiped! One might think it strange to worship when someone dies and so did David's household. They thought it strange that while his child was alive he did not eat, he wore sackcloth and ashes. But when the child was dead, he cleaned himself, ate and worshipped.

Sometimes when we are going through periods of our life when it seems God is punishing us for our wrong decisions, that does not mean He is not with us. God wants us to learn His truths, and yes, correction is never easy for the parent or the child. However, discipline is necessary to allow us to demonstrate our love and obedience to the Father. We should not confuse the two: discipline and punishment.

Only after his child's death did David learn truth. Scripture says: he comforted his wife Bathsheba and he went to her and lay with her and she gave birth to a son, and they named him Solomon, which means peace.

It also says that he later sent Nathan the prophet to David with the name Jedidiah, which means, loved by the Lord. The giving of this name suggests that the Lord's special favor rested on Solomon from his birth. And since the name also contained an echo of David's name, it provided assurance to David that the Lord also loved him and would continue his dynasty. See, the Lord knows the plans he has for us. That's why David could say: *"How precious to me are your thoughts, O God! How vast is the sum of them. You know when I sit and when I rise, you perceive my thoughts afar."*

I know that in spite of my sinful nature, God loves me. God knew He would send an angel into my hospital room to comfort me. The angel spoke these words: "God will give her back to you", speaking of my child. It was enough to make me rise off my bed of affliction. I knew I could not bring her back, but I would see her later if I committed my life to the one who gives life and sustains life.

David rose from his afflictions by fasting and weeping for his child, but more importantly he worshipped and gave the Lord reverence and asked, *"Where can I go from your presence Lord?"* We also should rise from our afflictions by asking the Lord: How can you be glorified in this? Where can I go from your presence Lord? David said: *" If I go to the heavens you are there; if I make my bed in the depths, you are there."*

After some years had passed, I made the decision to become a foster parent. At that time in history single parents weren't given the opportunity to be foster parents in North Carolina. But I knew God had extended His favor to me. I became one of the first in the state of North Carolina to be a licensed single family foster home. And I will never forget the day the social worker called me to tell me they had a child for me. How excited I was and at the same time a little disappointed because it wasn't an infant. I wanted a baby more than anything. But when this social worker called and said they had a three year old little girl, name Buttons. Of course I said a resounding YESSSSS.

How could I count the thoughts you have for me? The psalmist says: *"His thoughts for us outnumber the grains of sand. When I awake from counting the thoughts you are still with me."*

In spite of myself, God had given me a child to care for and I was as happy as could be. This little girl's nickname was "Buttons", and to tell you the truth she was just that. What a button she was, the prettiest eyes you every wanted to see. Just imagine looking at a garment with the prettiest buttons you have ever seen until you forget the garment and eventually all you can see are the buttons. Well, that is exactly what happened; I saw the prettiest eyes I had ever looked into along with a smile that would melt your heart. I forgot she was not a baby, the infant I so desperately wanted, but a three year old.

A couple of days later I was driving along thinking about all the things I would have to buy for my little girl; the bows, the matching socks and oh yeah, the little dresses with frilly ruffles. All of a sudden I heard a voice. I looked around, no one was in the car with me but this voice said to me, "you didn't thank me for her." Oh Boy! I had to pull over on the side of the road as I became overwhelmed with thanksgiving. I recognized the voice! It was the same voice as the angel from the hospital room.

Again I heard the voice say: 'you didn't thank me for her.' This most audible voice was so clear and distinct, but no one was in the car but me. Oh my God, I remembered what the angel had told me that lonely day in the hospital room that 'He would give her back to me.' He had given me back my little girl. She would have now been three years old. And the most amazing part was that when she turned seven years old I was able to adopt her. She had been born on Christmas day and her birth name was Iris. And because she did not have a middle name, I gave her my middle name, Ruth.

What a delight it was for all of us to have Iris. She shared the same birthday and learned early on who Jesus was. One of her first Christmas presents was an Easy Bake oven with which she made a Jesus birthday cake and we all sang to Him happy birthday. Iris still does this every year. I always make the distinction between the two birthdays and place great emphasis on God's presence because He gave her to me.

Shortly after my encounter of God's awesome presence in the car, I preached my first sermon at a rest home. It was titled: "Don't Forget to Say Thank You". As a child, I had no clue it was God's presence in my life allowing me the opportunities to seek Him and for giving me my parents to nurture me in the things of God. He has allowed me to experience His truths by demonstrating just how much He loves me. He disciplines me and lets me know that He will never leave me or forsake me, even when I'm wrong. His guidance leads us to paths of restoration, righteousness and redemption.

If there is anything I have learned it is that God takes His creation into places where eventually we recognize that He loves us and that He only wants our love in return. He will guide us into places where we begin to trust Him, love Him, and eventually know Him. If you love Him, you will obey Him. God's guidance is not an option in the believer's life.

His Presence

Teaches Us

"My son, do not despise the chastening of the Lord, nor be discouraged when you are rebuked by him: For whom the Lord loves he chastens, And scourges every son whom he receives. If you endure chastening, God deals with you as with sons; for what son is there whom a father does not chasten? But if you are without chastening, of which all have become partakers, then you are illegitimate and not sons. Furthermore, we have had human fathers who have corrected us, and we paid them respect. Shall we not much more readily be in subjection to the Father of spirits, and live? For they indeed for a few days chastened us as seemed best to them; but he for our profit, that we may be partakers of his holiness. Now no chastening seems to be joyful for the present, but painful: nevertheless, afterward it yields

*the peaceable fruit of righteousness to those who have been
trained by it." (Hebrews 12:5-11)*

Three kinds of disciplines are mentioned in the previous scripture. God will employ each one of these
to bring us into a place where our rebellion ceases and goes
from disobedience to obedience. Those that love Him will
obey Him. In the Greek translation of God's word we learn
that the word "scourges" means to flog or beat down, the
word "rebuked" means to verbally reprove or correct, and
the word "Chastening" means to instruct and teach.

What I have learned is this; my God will never leave me
nor forsake me. I realized this truth as I was coming through
one of those times in my life that I had to allow all that I
knew about God to consume me. This lesson began when I
made the decision to have gastric-bypass surgery. The doctor
I saw at the time lambasted me about my weight. He told
me I was looking at ten years to live at most, and that I was
looking at the possibility of a heart attack or stroke. It felt
like life had beaten me to the ground.

I was on my first initial visit with this doctor. I had just
been diagnosed with Type II Diabetes and was experiencing
elevated blood sugar and extreme chest pains. This new

doctor decided to call the ambulance after my E.K.G was abnormal. Here I was on my first visit and I was sent to the hospital by ambulance.

As a Physical Education teacher and coach I spent many years obese. My weight was around three hundred and seventeen pounds at the time. Every summer I would go on a crash diet and lose weight before the upcoming school year. However, on this particular summer it did not happen. My assigned schedule for the upcoming school year was Aerobics and Team Sports. I was the largest I had ever been in my life. Could you imagine me teaching aerobics let alone team sports? The previous school year I had been teaching Life Management Skills. My school however was up for SAC review and all teachers had to be teaching in their certified fields for the upcoming school year. Oh my, I really didn't know how I was going to do this but I knew I needed my job.

Because of my certification, I wasn't going to be allowed to teach Health Classes that year. After twenty four years of teaching combined in North Carolina and Florida, I had one of the greatest dilemmas of my life, so I thought.

That summer I had taken two courses to be certified in Life Management Skills but it wasn't enough credits for certification. That's when I saw the procedure for weight reduction in a nutrition textbook. The textbook had illustrations and explanations of Gastric Bypass procedures.

Shortly after that, I saw one of my co-workers at a check cashing store. She had lost a lot of weight and was looking really great. She told me she had gastric-bypass surgery and gave me the name of her doctor. The procedure she described was the same one I had read in the nutrition textbook. To make a long story short I went in for surgery and almost died. And because of the length of time it took to recuperate I was forced into retirement.

The recuperation process was a continuance of many years of suffering and I mean suffering. I lost everything; my career, my strength, my substance, my will and even my desire to live. And to top everything I went through, I lost all my retirement money. God used this flogging I endured to teach me to rely on His strength instead of relying on mine. Life, as I knew it, was gone. When you come to the end of yourself, there you will find God.

Another difficult lesson I learned is that when God speaks or rebukes us, we need to listen. Let me explain. I was doing some volunteer work at my church when a lady came in needing help. The church was already helping her with her rent. I got involved because her husband was sick and I was serving in Visitation Ministry. She seemed like a nice young lady, but when this nice young lady finished with me, the rest of my retirement money was gone and so was she. I was so amazed at the depth at which I had to learn this lesson. Here I was trying to help someone and she turned out to be a con-artist. Like most, we cry out WHY LORD. Instead, I cried out to God, "What is it you want me to learn from this, Lord?"

I partially told you how life had beaten me down, but what I didn't tell you is that the doctor whom performed the bypass-surgery BOTCHED IT UP. He had routed my intestine upside down. This resulted in vomiting my feces and I did not have a bowel movement for two and a half months. Needless to say, I almost died, one of my kidneys shut down. The doctor that worked to restore my kidneys explained to me that a reading of (6.0) was in the range for dialysis and here I was at (5.7).

I was gravely ill and all my vital organs were failing. The medical staff could not get a reading of my blood pressure nor start an IV because I was so severely dehydrated. The hospital staff doctor said that if I had stayed home one more day I would possibly be on dialysis the rest of my life. After all of this; hospitalizations, back to back surgeries, the gastric-bypass operation in August, and the corrective surgery in October, I had lost one hundred and eighty pounds. In the first month alone, I had lost one hundred pounds and almost lost my life. Because of my doctor's irresponsibility and negligence, I made the decision to take him to court.

The trial lasted for two weeks. And to tell you the truth, I felt I was the one on trial. I did, however, walk away with a very important lesson God wanted me to learn. It just so happens that during the time of the trial, I was reading Joel Osteen's book, 'Seven Steps to Living Your Best Life Now'. My sister kept insisting I needed to read Joel's book. But for some reason, I didn't pick up the book until the trial started. I discovered this book had a special anointing and I came through the trial knowing what God wanted me to learn; chastening. I needed to check my character, check my faith level and to walk in integrity and excellence. I came through all of that seeking God's purpose for my life with my whole heart. As difficult as it was, I could recognize the discipline I was going through as the Father's LOVE.

What a time in my life. When I started the malpractice trial I had ten dollars in my checking account. The time it took me to recuperate had forced me into retirement, ruined my life and now, I am the only living gastric-bypass surgery patient with a different procedure. The doctors that corrected the mistake had no other choice than to leave me like that. Basically I was left with nothing...humiliated, defeated, broke, and with a feeling of hopelessness.

It was so hard for me not to hate the doctor, the judge and the jury, the con-artist, not to mention the lawyer that defended the doctor. The only thing I could do was to leave it to God and allow Him and only Him to consume me. I had thoughts just like David, *"If only you would slay the wicked, O God! Away from me you blood thirsty men!" (Psalm 139: 19-22)* I also knew I needed to forgive them or my heavenly Father would not forgive me.

I had done some research before the trial on internet and found that this same doctor had performed surgery on a patient for Appendicitis. He lacerated her bladder in the process, repaired her bladder and left the diseased Appendix in. This patient almost died. The doctors that removed the diseased appendix discovered the repaired bladder. He was only reprimanded. Not only that, during the time of my trial, this doctor had five other lawsuits pending including one filed two days before mine. That's when I knew I had to stop him from hurting anyone else.

Some years ago I received a promise from God that I would become very wealthy; however, the money I was to receive was for End Time Harvest. I knew I would be obedient to God but how was I to convince my family and love ones of this promise. Some were already spending monies anticipating the outcome of the lawsuit.

I can attest to what Abram told the king of Sodom: *"I have raised my hand to the LORD, God Most High, the Possessor of heaven and earth, that I will take nothing, from a thread to a sandal strap, and that I will not take anything that is yours, lest you should say, 'I have made Abram rich"* *(Gen. 14: 22,23)*

The malpractice trial was not my source for the promise God gave me. God is the possessor of heaven and earth and I recognized that all we have comes from Him and Him alone. I can honestly say like Job; *"though He slay me, yet will I trust him." "I know my Redeemer lives, and that he shall stand at the latter day upon the earth."* I know that my God will be the one that gives me the ability to acquire wealth.

In scripture, Job was a just and upright man and honored God. He went through many tests and eventually had all restored to him, double when he prayed for his friends. I had experienced several tests before my malpractice trial. One took place as I was driving to the dentist. I was running late and while waiting at a red light, there was a man in a motorize wheelchair. His head was down and it did not look like he was moving. I was in such a hurry and I questioned my impulse to stop and help. However, I gave in to the prompting of being a Good Samaritan which I had just read in my daily devotions that morning.

As I drove away I increasingly became alarmed that perhaps he was not alive. I started to panic and at that moment, a lady I knew from a previous church I attended was pulling up to the traffic light. I called out to her and turned my car around. We both parked our cars, got out, and walked over to this man. She tapped his wheelchair and he opened his eyes and raised his head. Immediately I asked him if he was OK. With a radiant smile on his face and his countenance aglow, he answered yes and motored off. Almeta returned to her car and I left in mine. I had only driven less than a block when a voice told me to turn around. As I drove around the block I did not see him anywhere. The man had disappeared, and the same familiar voice said, "You passed the test."

I had another test while thrift shopping, which happens to be something I love to do. It would take too long to tell you all the details, but I found a very expensive watch and instead of keeping it, I explained its value to the shop owner and returned it to her. Again, I heard a voice tell me, I passed the test.

However, I also had tests where the Lord told me NOT to do something and I did it anyway. The Lord told me to not stop my tithes. Well I stopped sending the portion of my tithes to the District but I continued to bring my tithes to my local church. As a Minister, we are asked to pay 70 percent of our tithes to the District and 30 percent to the local congregation. After the malpractice case, in reflection, I realized that this was one test I did not pass. How could God trust me with millions? He has told me to tell my people that the tithe is holy unto the Lord.

This was a hard lesson to learn and I have since found out what being a true disciple really means. God said to me, "You are honoring me when you are obedient and bring a tenth of all." Any true disciple will not despise discipline and will remain teachable. In my obedience, I now share and proclaim the discipline of tithing as a chance to honor my Master.

Isaiah 48: 9-11 says: *"For My name's sake I will defer My anger, And for My praise I will restrain it from you, So that I do not cut you off. Behold, I have refined you, but not as silver; I have tested you in the furnace of affliction. For My own sake, for My own sake, I will do it; For how should My name be profaned? And I will not give My glory to another."*

Speaking of the furnace of affliction, the trial lasted approximately two weeks. On the last day, the judge asked the jury if they needed more time, it was around three o'clock on a Friday. If they had said they needed more time, they would have had to come back on Monday. The Judge made it clear he had an appointment he had to go to and could not stay to five o'clock. Lord, please have mercy, I need your mercy Lord, over and over I pleaded, please have mercy LORD. The talking ceased in the room where the jurors were and the verdict came back NOT GUILTY. I looked at the other lawyer and the doctor and their mouths were wide open in disbelief. They themselves could not believe they had won. As strange as it sounds, that's when I knew that my God had protected me and that His grace is sufficient for me. He was with me throughout the whole thing.

The doctor who testified as an expert in my case was the one who repaired the botched surgery. He said he had to stand over me an hour just to figure out how to put me back together. The defendant's doctor expert, which by the way was paid thirty-five thousand dollars and had never done one of these procedures unassisted, testified that if I had been left like I was after the bypass surgery, I would have been dead in three days. The doctors that testified on my behalf did not receive any payment for their testimonies.

At one point during the trial, Doctor Gonzales, the one who repaired the botched surgery, stepped down from the witness stand and gave me a kiss on the check, the defendant's attorney immediately demanded a mistrial. She kept demanding mistrial for everything, and because of this, the judge had to make rulings three or more times each day. It was difficult for my attorney to present my case.

It was so hard sitting in the courtroom as I witnessed my life in totality on trial. I had to sit through the lies and hear the partial truths that were questioning my integrity. If only I had been given a little time to expound upon what was said, it all would have given truthful insight and understanding. You can imagine how difficult it was for me to endure this every day. During the whole trial my attorney had instructed me when to be there and when to stay home. For this I am very thankful, I did not have to sit there listening to half truths or outright lies everyday of the trial. On the days I did attend, it was very humbling. I had to control myself from screaming out 'liars, why don't you tell the whole truth'.

So many injustices occurred during the trial. This courtroom happened to be a very small space and because of the size, we did not have much room to bring in my attorney's presentations. In addition to the space limitations, there were also too many objections and declarations of mistrial brought up daily by the other attorney. Often the displays were delayed or completely overlooked.

On one particular day, as our medical expert was testifying about my past and present physical condition, right in the middle of his testifying, the judge called for a recess. It was time for lunch. And he could not wait until this witness finished? After lunch, one of the ladies that worked for my attorney, the person that had been working on my entire medical history from birth, was sitting in the waiting room next to my sister and myself. The medical expert who had previously been testifying was sitting near her. They began talking about special needs children since they both had personal firsthand experiences with these children. They were just sharing and talking with each other on personal ways they handled situations. As they continued conversing, in walks the defense attorney for the doctor. By the look on her face and the stride in her walk, she was very upset they were talking and she demanded an audience with the judge. She made known what she thought she saw and had witnessed outside in the waiting area. When the court trial resumed, it had become a situation that if God didn't intervene, all would be lost.

It was praying time and I knew it so well! The worker and the medical expert were facing a very difficult situation that could have cost the trial. "Oh my gracious Lord," I pleaded. "Please have mercy for their sakes." There I sat between two attorneys and the Holy Spirit was prompting me to pray in the spirit. I don't remember how long I was praying in unknown tongues, but I was praying my all, spirit to spirit, to my Creator. As I was petitioning for supernatural intervention in this dilemma, the attorneys sitting on both sides of me did not react. And I assumed they also were praying as well. Oh how our God moved mightily and all went well. How grateful I was that the judge ruled in our favor and that our God moves mightily. Hallelujah, and I give Him the glory.

Most afternoons after returning from lunch, several of the jurors would nod out and have a hard time staying awake. As for me, I was physically there, but most of the time I was experiencing and reliving 'the vision'. It was during this trial that I was being restored and refreshed, right there in the courtroom. As the trial was unfolding, the things that had been shown to me so many years in advance were brought to my attention. I believe the vision had been stirred up and reoccurring because, as I said before, it was as if I were being put on trial instead of the doctor. I don't understand this, but every time I looked to my right at the man who had destroyed my life so to speak, I saw a man that was so downcast that I began feeling sorry for him. It was extremely hard to watch and hear the things said against me, yet I could not comment. But what I find even stranger is that I began to lose my desire to fight back.

When I was finally called to the witness stand I was so nervous. I had been given so many directives as to what not to say and what to say. I felt very insecure and totally help-less so I just kept answering the attorney's questions with, "All I wanted was for him to help me. I was so sick." The attorney became so insistent that the judge ordered me to answer her questions. Again, I could not answer her. This time I said, "I felt like my life was leaving my body and my family was there watching and they equally felt hope-less." While I was inside that courtroom, none of my family members were present to support me. The courtroom was too small, no one else was allowed inside. However, God did not leave me alone. He sent one of my family members who worked for the court system and was in charge of all the clerks. As I was taking the witness stand, he walked in. It was such a support to see Ray sitting there and that he was able to go and tell my family how I was doing. They were all waiting and sitting outside in the waiting area.

As I stepped down from the witness stand feeling broken and defeated, I could sense evil forces at work all around us. The spiritual forces of evil were working in overdrive, pulling out all the stops. The doctor's attorney began to present her defense. She called in my primary physician to the stand by name. However, another person walked up and took the witness stand instead of my doctor. I was guessing it was someone from the insurance company reading my doctors deposition. She proceeded to question him. As I told you earlier, for some reason my primary physician was not very cooperative with my attorney. In spite of everything that was happening, God gave me a song in my heart. Throughout the whole process and afterwards I sang it over and over in my mind, "Your grace is sufficient for me." I know I would have surely fainted and I'm so grateful for His strength.

These two weeks seemed like a life time. Everything his attorney presented about me was either embellished or fabricated and his attorney had gleaned information from my very own deposition. Words from my own mouth were used against me. As an example, they tried to use the social security disability denial as part of the trial record. My attorney did not want this to be admitted due to some medical information. Information about the mental hospital, Mercy hospital, my miscarriage and abortion were included and my attorney had fought hard not to include them in the trial. I coincidently received a call during the trial, from the attorney who handled the appeal process. I was indeed granted social security disability. So during lunch time, I went to obtain this information so that I could give it to my attorney just in case the defending attorney decided to use this against me.

God showed me that His grace is truly sufficient. He made sure to let me know everything was going to be well even after I lost the malpractice lawsuit.

The doctors that repaired the surgery and saved my life repeatedly reassured me that I would be under their care and that they would supervise this procedure from here on out. Also, the State of Florida contacted me and asked me if they could use my case in their endeavor to look into the other cases filed against this same doctor. It seems the State of Florida follows up on doctors that have four or more lawsuits filed against them. It made me feel so good to know that God's grace is sufficient. He kept the doctor and myself whole during the trial. However, He is and remains a Righteous Judge, "Vengeance is mine sayeth the Lord". It was a very hard way to learn what He needed to teach me. My desire is to always remain pliable and teachable in His hands, for He is the Master.

The defense attorney was a female as aggressive as a viper. The judge made several trivial rulings because of her demands for mistrial. The doctor that testified on my behalf was not allowed to eat lunch with us. The Psychologist that testified in my case said, "My God woman," as he spoke to the doctor's attorney. Again the judge had to make another ruling, that God's name could not be used.

On one morning of the trial, the doctor's attorney complained about a run in her panty-hose. Jokingly the judge asked her if she wanted a mistrial for the run in the panty hose. It was ridiculous just how many declarations of mistrials the judge had to rule on. The sad part of it all is that we would not have even been there if this doctor would have just come to the hospital to help figure out what was wrong with me.

I recall one hospital stay that lasted seventeen days. And the only reason I was released was because I started concealing my vomiting to avoid the injections, I wanted to go home. Another hospital stay lasted thirty plus days and I only saw this doctor twice. He came in one time because the line in my groin area was not working and he had to put a central line in. The second time was because the admitting doctor demanded he come in. He sat on my bed beside me and said he was ordering some tests.

I was not a pretty sight to look at, I had tubes running everywhere. I had feeding tubes and a tube in my nose running to my stomach to help stop the vomiting. At one point I remember asking the nurse to please leave the stomach tube in. Now, anyone who has ever had one of these tubes running down their nose and all the way to their stomach knows how uncomfortable and painful this is. And here I was begging to keep it in! Since the surgery I had been vomiting constantly. For two months everything including my saliva would go down mix with bile and come back up.

I did not have solid food for thirty days, nothing by mouth. It took the hospital two weeks to stabilize me before they could open me up for exploratory surgery so that they could determine what exactly was going on. They knew something was terribly wrong.

On one visit to the emergency room my vomiting alarmed the whole staff. That night during the changing of shifts in the ER, a doctor passing through commented to the nurses, "Someone let one go." He meant that someone had a bowel movement but the nurses told him that the smell was my vomit. His reply back was, "If that is so then that's feces."

One of my soccer moms worked at the hospital and helped to take care of me. I asked her if one of her children I taught and coached could come and visit me. She kindly said, "Coach Washington, I don't want Crystal to see you like this, wait until you are better."

I don't know how to begin to describe the suffering I endured for those two weeks of my life as I was on trial instead of the doctor. I was defenseless with each lie after lie. Oh what a wounded soul I was when I turned and saw the doctor rejoicing in my pain. As I stepped out of that court-room I let out one of the most blood curling screams anyone could ever imagine hearing. My poor sister did not know what to do. There I was on the floor screaming at the top of my lungs and there they were rejoicing in my hurt, they were rejoicing in my pain.

But it didn't stop here. After I lost the case this doctor decided to sue me. It's hard to believe, I was being sued for attempting to stop this doctor from possibly killing someone else. Yes, that's right, the doctor demanded I pay him for what it cost to defend himself in the lawsuit. It's called Tax of Cost. He also wanted me to pay him eight thousand dollars for a display board they created to display all the hurts and pains in my life from adulthood on. They had even displayed my mother and father's death on a chart. This chart had red marks by everything they thought had caused me stress.

I never really grieved my mother's death. It was very hard for me to have my mother's death on the display board. I was that one family member that tried to hold everything together for the others. I was the one who took care of all the funeral arrangements and other businesses, while at the same time keep my own sanity. Now, twenty years later, in the middle of this trial, I found myself grieving my mother's death, my best friend's death for the first time.

I know God allowed me to not win the lawsuit. I would have been so distracted with that amount of money.

Regardless of what was happening, that's when I knew that my God truly loved me. Here I was able in His strength to get up off that floor and walk out of that courthouse without being arrested for causing a scene. All types of officers showed up to escort me out, and of course the judge had to leave, so he too was escorted to his vehicle. I know it was God's sustaining presence that kept me from completely losing my mind and this time taking a legitimate trip to the mental hospital.

The trial ended on a Friday and my church had service on Friday night. I will never ever forget the praise team singing that night. I am free to run, I am free to dance, I am free to live for you, I am free. I ran all around the church that night and finally collapsed on the altar right before my God. That's where I've been ever since, seeking His Presence.

I was finally free to live for Him. Those four years of my life were consumed with the lawsuit, doctor appointments, psychologist and psychiatrist. I had to make several trips to Shane hospital in Gainesville, Florida to see a specialist because the vomiting and diarrhea would not stop. I quickly became a size four all the way down from a size 26 plus.

I was having a difficult time getting over the trial. I continued reliving it over and over again in my mind, all the lies that were told, the things that should have been said, but weren't. I couldn't stop retrying the case over and over, my thoughts were consumed. And at the same time, I had to walk in new instruction, the chastening of the Lord. I needed to check my character, faith level and to continue to walk in integrity and excellence, all while continuing to remain teachable. I remember thinking and asking God; "Please give your beloved rest, oh my God, please help me to stop reliving this trial. "

As I told you earlier, I write when I can't do anything physically to stop the madness. So I wrote a letter to the doctors that testified in my case, the ones that repaired the surgery. And I thanked them for being men of excellence because they didn't have to do it. And because of what they did, my faith in the medical profession was restored.

The letter I wrote to the doctors:

April 6, 2006

Dr. Gonzalez, Dr. Rabaza:

I wanted to write this letter to personally thank you for saving my life and being men of integrity. I know the truth and God Almighty knows that I'm alive today because of your intervention, for you could have elected not to get involved.

I will be eternally grateful to the both of you for standing on the truth in that travesty of justice. Because of the both of you, I'm able to believe in the medical profession again. He won the case, but I won the spiritual battle. I'm Alive!

I will always remember your personal sacrifices that both of you made on my behalf. I will pray always for you, your practice and families, that God will reward you abundantly.

Thank you and Thank you, for being men of integrity, and for the excellence and caring for your patient's total wellbeing.

Thank You Always,

Next I wrote a letter to Willie Gary and Larry Williams, both are attorneys I went to school with in North Carolina.

Both were fellow Shaw University students who took the case. I thanked them for allowing God's grace to assist me in the malpractice suit. I wanted to encourage them to let the "Wings of Justice" to keep flying, that's the name of the firm's airplane.

In the letter to Mr. Gary I wrote:

April 6, 2006

Mr. Willie Gary,

As I sit here pondering the goodness of God, I just wanted to write and thank you personally for allowing the Father to use you. THANK YOU for taking my case and for caring for the oppressed. God sees your efforts and will reward you.

I could not have received a more Caring and Professional service anywhere. Continue to walk in Integrity and Excellence, because that is what is required of us all.

Mr. Gary, I can't tell you how gracious the measure of God's grace has been, even in losing the case. I don't even view it as a loss, because I won the spiritual battle. First of all, I'm alive! Secondly, I'm sad but joy will come in the morning. Thirdly, God's light is still aglow after all the suffering and pain not to mention the travesty of justice. I can only say this for I know the Righteous Judge. Although justice did not prevail in this case, I'm praying God please let the truth be revealed.

Words aren't enough to THANK YOU! I will continue to pray for the firm, you and your family. May everything you touch prosper for seed time and harvest is the key to success.

My Great Uncle Wilbert Taylor sowed a seed three genera-
tions ago and I'm reaping a harvest now. Oh, How Amazing!

Willie, I am so proud of you. My prayer will always be
"FATHER, LET THE WINGS OF JUSTICE KEEP FLYING
UNTIL YOU RETURN."

Thank You Always,

My great uncle was a blessing to Mr. Gary when he
was a young man working in the cane fields in Belle Glade,
Florida. When Willie purposed in his heart to better him-
self, my Great Uncle Wilbert Taylor sowed a seed in young
Willie's life and he left Belle Glade and started college in
North Carolina.

My sister Marilyn also went to college at Shaw University
and she was the one that contacted Larry Williams about the
lawsuit against the doctor that botched the surgery. At first, I
think the firm took the case based on my great uncle's sowing
in Willie's life. It is hard to get doctors to testify against
another doctor. Later, I found out from Mr. McManus, my
attorney in the case, that they were relieved that Dr. Gonzalez
would testify to the fact of how he found me and what he had

to do to save my life. Initially none of my doctors were cooperating especially my primary physician.

I wanted to personally thank Mr. McManus my attorney, so I placed a call to his office. I was told he wasn't in the office and had not been in the office since the trial ended. The office reached him and he returned my call. Mr. McManus was so depressed, he told me he could not eat or sleep since the trial. He also said that this trial was the worst travesty of justice he had witnessed in his thirty some years of law practice.

Being the encourager I am, I wrote him this letter:

April 18, 2006

Mr. Mc Manus,

Thank you, Thank You! Oh, how I thank God for you. I'm writing this letter of encouragement to express my gratitude to you personally. After our phone conversation I felt as though there was no doubt that I had the best representation. Continue to stand for right, because so many need you. Never let the roaring lion rob you of your joy. The Lion of Judah is still King of Kings.

I will never forget your time and efforts and especially how you protected my character. (Not to have the abortion brought, or the miscarriage, into the trial.) Although we lost the case, I do not accept it as a defeat because I asked my Heavenly Father to reveal to me what he wanted me to learn during the trial.

The Almighty did just that. He said to me, "Carolyn I want you to walk in integrity, excellence and faith, and check your character." Let me comfort you if you viewed that trial as a loss. It wasn't easy, but it was necessary in order for me to deal with certain aspects of my life, especially all of the disappointments.

If I could tell you how rich I am for having endured it. All the fruit of the Spirit were evident during, and will continue in my life, after this trial; (PEACE, MEEKNESS, TEMPERANCE, LONG SUFFERING, GENTLENESS and FAITH.)

Mr. McManus, when you have done all you know to stand, stand anyhow. Sometimes the great things in life aren't measured in treasures of this earth. The greatest treasure is to TRUST in the Almighty who made the earth and everything that dwells therein. Never allow yourself to become weary in well-doing. The oppressed need attorneys like you.

The times we are living in dictate a lot of injustices, but always remember we aren't governed by this world system. All who witnessed that travesty of justice are asking when does justice prevail? I submit to you; justice prevails when you did what you did for me, walking in faith, knowing that even when we don't win. He is and will always be the Righteous Judge.

I will be eternally grateful to God that you were my attorney in this case. I just wanted you to know that I witnessed the evidence of the presence of the fruit of the Spirit in your life, which allowed me to endure. My prayers continue for you. I'm asking the Father to give you, his servant, rest and to restore unto you all and help you realize that God has even greater things in store for you.

May God Bless You,

Mr. McManus wrote me a thank you card, thanking me for the letter of encouragement. He said and I quote: "Thanks for your kind letter. In 33 years of legal practice, I have received very few thank you letters, and none so inspiring. May God bless you in ways only God can imagine." I wasn't thanking him so much as encouraging him that God had more in store for him. And, at the same time, encouraging myself like David did in the Lord.

I had so many people watching me to see my reaction during and after the trial. During the trial I was actually praying for the doctor that put me there. I prayed he wouldn't get sick or have a heart attack. His countenance was so downcast I kind of felt sorry for him. It was my understanding from my physiatrist that this doctor had lost his daughter in a car accident before the trial. He had also gotten divorced in the investigating stages of the trial.

After the trial no one could believe he had won. My attorney, Mr. McManus, informed me that the Law firm would not pursue it any further. It had cost them hundreds of thousands of dollars up to that point. And I was informed that Mr. Willie Gary had absorbed the cost of trial personally. So there was no way I would go forth with any more of this madness, I'd had enough.

I just wanted my life back and all of the madness to cease. It was very difficult to stop trying the case in my mind. I needed to demonstrate God's fruit of the Spirit, so many were watching my reactions. But God assured me of His presence over and over, especially when he allowed me to write the letter to the doctor. I was unable to mail this letter because of the lawsuit he now is pursuing against me.

April 18, 2006

Dr._____,

First of all you might find this letter unusual coming from me, but I meant you no harm, never could I ever wish any harm to anyone. I'm writing this letter to thank you. Sounds strange, however it's true, those who are in Christ Jesus are peculiar.

What happened to me was real, the pain and suffering, but what happened during the trial birthed new revelations in my life. All of it was a misfortune but necessary for me to grow spiritually. If I told you I prayed harder for you than I did for the outcome of the trial, it would seem unreal. The truth is I continue to pray for you.

The same God that helped me to endure is the God that will see you through too. I'm laughing now, because I'm blessed to be alive and no harm came to either of us in spite of the misfortune. Dr._____ as I reflect back to the trial and what I learned, it is immeasurable to what I could have hoped to gain if I had won.

I know you never meant me any harm. Sometimes when we set our focus on earthly treasures it can deceive us, by allowing us to do things that are uncommon to man. It is our nature to love and help others, but when we allow greed to be our focus, we cease loving and helping others.

I also am aware that you are going through quite a lot, divorce, the loss of your daughter and other misfortunes. God Almighty knows and cares for you. Cast all your cares upon him for he cares for you. I pray the blessings of the Lord will allow you a way of escape and heal all your hurt and pain.

This misfortune left me depleted in earthly treasures, but I'm rich in love, peace, meekness, and temperance and long suffering.

May God Bless You,

I was convicted about giving the doctor's name. As I was blessing him one day, God spoke to me and said STOP, you don't really mean this. So on that day, I stopped blessing this doctor. I thought I was doing what God's word tells us we're supposed to do. Aren't we asked to bless our enemy? But God, let me know I had not truly forgiven the doctor, the lawyer, or the judge. Yes, I had forgiven them verbally, but it wasn't in my heart. I realized I would not be forgiven if I did not forgive those that caused me so much pain. Prior to this, I would tell anyone who would listen, about what happened to me and what this awful doctor did. And because I had lost so much weight, I had more than a willing audience to listen.

I also stopped giving out any names, nor do I tell people what happened to me, unless I'm prompted to share by the Holy Spirit, like right now. However, I still never give his name. I wrote the following poem as part of my forgiveness process. It wasn't until I truly forgave everyone that had a part in this travesty, could I then truly rejoice. You see, I needed the Father's forgiveness for my sins. When any of us hold on to our misfortunes and prolong letting go, it only hinders us, not the people or the misfortunes that have caused us pain. Now, I can bless the doctor, God knows I truly mean it. It was during this time that "No Forgiveness, No Home Here" was birthed.

No Forgiveness, No Home Here

Oh, how you long to have control of me.

Yet, your venomous poison can't find a home.

God's love for all abides here.

Oh, how you long to envelope my thoughts.

Yet, your consistency must cease.

God's peace abides here.

Oh, how you long for me to relinquish my authority.

Yet, I long to see Jesus, therefore He is in control.

God's grace abides always here.

I entered this poem in a contest. It was my first published poem. I trust one day it will be the will of God that the letter I wrote makes it into the hands of the doctor and I still continue to say, bless him Father, with no malice in my heart, bless the young lady that needed my help, bless the judge and the jury, Father, and most of all the attorney for the doctor.

God did have greater things in store for Mr. McManus, my attorney. He later was appointed judge by the governor of his state. I'm so grateful I was able to take my eyes off the circumstances and ask God what He wanted to teach me through all of this.

God will never leave you nor forsake you, I tell you. Months after the trial I was volunteering at the church where I attended when a copy machine representative came into the office to sell the church a copier. I was sitting at the reception desk answering the phone when he walked in. I sensed immediately in my spirit that God wanted to speak to me through the man sitting there waiting on the church's Office Manager. But we just politely chatted about the weather and the goodness of God. The copy machine representative never did say anything, even though I sensed he had a word from the Lord for me.

Through everything I had gone through, I was determined not to allow the flogging, rebuking and chastising I endured to rob me of God's presence. At that time I was feeling as low as you could feel without fainting and giving up. I stood firm on the word and let the peace of God that surpasses all understanding rule my heart.

As a new creature, God had redefined me: *"Therefore, as the elect of God, holy and beloved, put on tender mercies, kindness, humility, meekness, long suffering; bearing with one another, and forgiving one another, if anyone has a complaint against another; even as Christ forgave you, so you also must do. But above all these things put on love which is the bond of perfection. And let the peace of God rule in your hearts, to which also you were called in one body, and be thankful. Let the word of Christ dwell in you richly in all wisdom, teaching and admonishing one another in psalms and hymns and spiritual songs, singing with grace in your hearts to the Lord." (Colossians 3:12-16)*

That evening I left the church after volunteering, still determined to keep my joy. I was full of determination. My God had brought me through the botched surgery, through one of the worst travesties of justice in the malpractice lawsuit and He kept me sane even after the loss of my retirement money to the con-artists.

I know I can rely on his mercy, just like David was crying out in (Psalm 51:1-4). *"Have mercy on me O God according to your unfailing love; according to your great compassion blot out my transgressions. Wash away all my iniquity and cleanse me from my sin. For I know, my transgressions and my sin is always before me. Against you, you only, have I sinned and done what is evil in your sight, so that you are proved right when you speak and justified when you judge."* It was against God that I had sinned. I had to repent for altering God's creation. Having the surgery altered what God had perfectly designed. God tells us that; *"We are fearfully and wonderfully made; your works are wonderful, I know that full well."* (Psalm 139:14) And, although I was giving freely, I was not listening to God when He was speaking, telling me where to sow. God also tells us that; *"My sheep know my voice and they obey me."* O God, I cried out. Have mercy on me.

Not long after, a prophet came to town and visited our church. He gave me a word concerning what had gone on with the con-artist. I don't know who could have told him. I was personally too embarrassed to tell anyone, including my family. The prophet directly said this to me, "God has given you the compassion to give, and He wants to fine tune your gift of giving." This is a gift and it requires that I listen to Him before I go and bless others. God might be working in the other person's life and I indirectly might be hindering what God is trying to accomplish. I can't keep rescuing others when God is breaking them.

You know what God did. The next day I returned to the church to volunteer. Clara, the Pastor's secretary told me that someone had left something for me. It was a folded piece of paper. I opened it and to my amazement God was speaking in my circumstances and it was a page out of the bible copied with the scripture verse, Hebrew 13:5, blocked out and part of it highlighted. *"Let your character or moral disposition be free from love of money including greed, avarice, lust, and craving for earthly possessions and be satisfied with your present circumstances and with that you have;*

for He Himself has said, I will not in any way fail you nor give you up nor leave without support. "I will not, I will not, I will not in any degree leave you helpless nor forsake nor let you down [relax my hold on you]. Assuredly not!" (The Amplified Bible)

I carry that folded piece of paper in my bible to this day to remind me of His presence and to what extent God will go to reveal He cares and that He will never leave us. As I read it I started crying because He had heard my cry. Clara didn't have a clue what was going on or why I was crying. When I asked her who left this for me, she said it was the copier machine representative I had seen the day before. I knew he had something to tell me that same day but didn't. After I left the church He had copied this page out of the bible and highlighted and blocked out what God wanted him to tell me. He then left it with the pastor's secretary to give to me. I never saw him again.

The lesson was learned that day and oh how grateful I am he does not leave us in our mess. It's important that we learn these lessons quickly or we will wander blindly until we have to experience a Damascus road experience like Saul. God's truths are revelation truths and until we learn them we are blind to His all loving Presence. *"As he jour-*

neyed he came near Damascus, and suddenly a light shone around him from heaven. Then he fell to ground, and heard a voice saying to him, 'Saul, Saul, why are your persecuting Me?" (Acts 9)

Only after Saul was obedient to the voice of God and responded to the vision, was his sight restored. Verse 19 says;" *he had received food and was strengthened."* After Saul spent some days with the disciples at Damascus; *"he immediately began to preach the Christ in the synagogues, that Jesus is the Son of God."*

Like Saul, I had a revelation of truth to who the Son of God is in my life and what His presence means. All the people that had witnessed God strengthening me through these ordeals were amazed. To tell you the truth I never could have made it without his strength. Now every morning I rise, I seek His strength and seek His face [His presence]. Psalms 105:4

His Presence

Leads Us

After receiving the scripture from the copy machine sales representative, I knew then and there that God cares and when He speaks we are to listen. No one can make me doubt that God will never leave me nor forsake me. That day the significance and importance of His presence became so very real to me. All my life He has been there, even as a child. But now I have learned to totally trust Him.

God's word declares He is a very present help, and we can boldly come to him in times of trouble and find help when we need it. Mercy and grace is there to help us through those times when we aren't aware of His Presence. I will never take for granted His precious sacrifice. *"Let us then approach the throne of grace with confidence, so that we may receive mercy and find grace to help us in our time of need." (Hebrew 4:16)*

When God is leading us one way and we become impatient or when He is providing for us and we complain, we are taking His presence for granted just like the children of Israel when they complained against God and Moses.

"They traveled from Mount Hor along the route to the Red Sea to go around Edom. But the people grew impatient on the way; they spoke against God and against Moses, and said, "Why have you brought us up out of Egypt to die in the desert? There is no bread. There is no water. And we detest this miserable food." The Lord then sent venomous snakes among them. They bit the people and many Israelites died. The people then came to Moses repentant saying, "We sinned when we spoke against the Lord and against you. Pray the Lord will take the snakes away from us." So Moses prayed for the people. The Lord said to Moses, "Make a snake put it up on a pole; anyone who is bitten can look at it and live." So Moses made a bronze snake and put it up on a pole. Then when anyone was bitten by a snake and looked at the bronze snake, he lived. (Numbers 21: 4- 9)

When I was in seminary and my mother became ill, I recall complaining and questioning God as to why I had to move back to Miami, Florida. My situation ended up being worse than the children of Israel in the desert when the Lord sent venomous snakes among them. I was having a difficult time making a decision to leave everything; my career, my church family, my home, and divinity school. I ended up fasting for thirty days without food or water, as I sought God's leading and direction.

I had completed 45 semester hours of Divinity School and I only needed 65 hours to complete my Masters. The program required me to give up every Saturday for two years from 8 o'clock in the morning to 5 o'clock in the evening. I had come this close to graduating and now I had to leave. A lot of time was spent complaining and asking God, Why?

Strange things started happening as I fasted for that long a period time, without food or water. I experienced and lived a vision and words will never be adequate enough to describe the things I experienced and saw. This all started because I could not make a decision and trust God's leading.

I remember doing things, hearing things and speaking out all that I saw. Each time I was shown a new part of the vision, I would call my mom to tell her. It was when I told her

I heard the trumpet sounding, that she became increasingly alarmed. Since she could not get to me quick enough from Miami, she called the local authorities in North Carolina for assistance. When the police arrived they were unsure of what to do with me. First they took me to the jail and later to a woman's facility. After what seemed to be a couple of hours, I ended up at Doretha Dix mental hospital in Raleigh, North Carolina. It was at this hospital that my open vision continued.

During this vision, immediately after the trumpet had sounded, I was called up into heaven. It was at this time that I had to give an account of all the deeds I had done throughout my life. I saw all the faces of the children I could have witnessed to but didn't. I was remorseful and grieving saying over and over again just how sorry I was that I did not yield to His leading. These were not only the children that I didn't witness to but also the ones I had unintentionally hurt through word or deed. I continued asking for forgiveness, pleading for another chance to correct my actions and to tell them about Jesus.

Nothing, and I mean, absolutely nothing had escaped His notice, especially my very thoughts. In heaven our thoughts are greatly magnified before our all knowing, all wise and all powerful Authority. Imagine your thoughts echoing across every mountain top and every valley below as if they were shouted. My thoughts were even louder than any words could possibly be shouted on earth. Our thoughts in heaven are instantly recognized and realized the moment they happen. I also could sense the intensity of my motives and wanted nothing more than to return back to earth to tell others about the awesomeness of God's glorious presence. I could not escape Him and all that was within me wanted nothing more than for everyone to know the revelation revealed to me.

With this overwhelming first hand revelation of His awesomeness and of His presence, I have an urgency to tell everyone how relevant and how important it is to seek His presence with all that you are and in all that you do. It is essential or should I say…It is a MUST!

Before all this began I recall, while studying in seminary, God drawing me closer to Himself. His words were so sweet and all so enlightening. I desired and began to ask for the mind of Christ. Not knowing the ramification of my desire, I spent many days on a fast mediating and hungering for truth and understanding about the things of God. I believe God had me walk through this long journey to see as He saw. It was during the vision and before I heard the trumpet sound, that God allowed me to supernaturally see the many injustices that had and were occurring around me.

As I stood at the judgment seat of believers, my life unfolded every personal act of my unrighteousness I had ever done. Everything had been recorded and my life was on display, opened up and spread out before me, one segment at a time. Every detail of my life was moving rather quickly and all I could do was weep as every word, deed and action quickly flashed before me. My posture, attitudes and dispositions were also on display as well. I kept uncontrollably sobbing with the realization of this all so powerful truth in it's wholeness. Our God is a powerful and Righteous Judge.

His full wonder, glorious power, might, wisdom, understanding, knowledge and council was on display as the One who reigns in majesty, with supreme authority and rule. I did not look nor could I see. But I did sense that I was bowing before, the all Righteous, all Powerful Judge. I knew His eyes were ablaze and every injustice was being consumed in this glorious presence and all seeing eyes. Then I saw restitution taking place for all my injustices, all the ones shown before me as I stood before Him and wept. I was being restored and my restoration was complete in Him. That's when the all powerful truth became so very prominent. He was truly the

Righteous Judge and our restitution and restoration can only be complete by His Spirit. He promises to pour out in the last days upon all flesh and this will only be accomplished by His presence and the empowering of the Spirit of God in us.

"The hands of Zerubbabel Have laid the foundation of this temple; Then you will know That the LORD of hosts has sent Me to you. For who has despised the day of small things? For these seven rejoice to see the plumb line in the hand of Zerubbabel. They are the eyes of the LORD. Which shall scan to and fro throughout the whole earth." Zechariah 4: 9-10

Zechariah who's name means Yahweh remembers, reminds me of what He said in (Matt. 25:21) in the parable of the talents; *"His lord said to him, Well done, good and faithful servant; you were faithful over a few things, I will make you ruler over many things. Enter into the joy of your lord."* I'm so glad He allowed me to return so I could emphasize the importance of letting faith arise in our hearts. We must always remember that things are not always as they seem. Everything we do in this life WILL be judged. When the Israelites faithfully completed the second temple, it may have seemed small to them, but everything in this life whether it is great or small, good or bad will stand before Him at the judgment seat. This judgment will not be to determine whether we belong there or not, it is for determining the extent of our rewards and I knew this as I stood before Him. The Righteous Judge was looking ahead to his glorious Bride which is spread out amongst the nations and filled with the explosive power of His Holy Spirit. He so desires to reveal His wonderful glorious presence throughout the earth and continues to draw all who would believe in HIM. *"Concerning the gospel they are enemies for your sake, but concerning the election they are beloved for the sake of the fathers. For the gifts and the calling of God are irrevocable."* *Romans 11:28-29.*

After years of discouragement, Zerubbabel governor of Judah is assured that he will see the fulfillment of God's purpose for him. Today God's glorious Bride, the church, is still being built. We must do our part to pray and work in faith so that all will come the know Jesus as Messiah, the One pierced for our very own sin. All the while our expectation needs to be full as we look with hope to the glorious return of our risen Savior.

Look in faith towards the Day of the LORD. In faith I had asked to see through his eyes and this is what He showed me. We should continuously be asking the Father to pour out His Spirit so that the world will know that out of His loving heart, Jesus died for our right to stand before Him at the Judgment Seat. As we are faithful in a little, God likewise can entrust us with more. I could not understand the depth of this revelation until He revealed himself to me and my response was that of obedience. Let Him reveal himself to you and respond in obedience.

As I stood at the judgment seat I fully understood that His stance was the glory being revealed that was tried by fire. Here I was before the glorious presence of the spotless King of Kings, He without sin, the wonderful matchless SON of God. As I stood before Him, I was sensing all of His strength and endurance, along with the harshness of recompense for my personal iniquities and transgression along with those of the whole world. The only reason I stood there and could stand there to be judged was because He was victorious.

"Because He has appointed a day on which He will judge the world in righteousness by the Man whom He has ordained.

He has given assurance of this to all by raising Him from the dead." Acts 17:31

Praise God it was for love's sake that justice was released and we have the favor of God, released in the form of abundant blessings and Grace. I, Carolyn Ruth Washington was able to stand before the Righteous Judge. The magnitude of this blows me away! In total oneness I was at the mighty glory of the ONE who was empowered to carry this great burden for mankind with much authority for love's sake. My joy was and is that of elation that He had paid the price and paid it in full. Nothing is more humbling than to stand before the Almighty knowing what you really deserve. I knew without a doubt that the only reason I was there was because of the paid price for my undeserved redemption.

Look to Jesus who, as both Priest and King, carries God's glory. You need to understand that as the body of Christ, we have been made a king and a priest. YOU HAVE BEEN CALLED TO RULE AND ALSO REIGN WITH HIM and to carry the glory that was on display. We all should be asking the Lord daily to conform us to the image of His glorious Son and to actively seek to be like Jesus; as we extend salvation to the world with humility and love.

"Then Jesus cried out and said, He who believes in Me, believes not in Me but in Him who sent Me. And he who sees me sees Him who sent Me. I have come as a light into the world, that whoever believes in Me should not abide in darkness. And if anyone hears My words and does not believe, I do not judge him; for I did not come to judge the world but to save the world. He who rejects Me, and does not receive My words, has that which judges him- the word that I have spoken will judge him in the last day. For I have not spoken on My own authority; but the Father who sent me gave me a command, what I should say and what I should speak. And I know that His command is everlasting life. Therefore, whatever I speak, just as the Father has told Me, so I speak."
John 12: 44-50 NKJV

I knew as I stood there, that my sins were truly forgiven and that I stood in the presence of the ONE who allowed His BLOOD to be shed for me so that I could be standing there. An overwhelming peace came upon me and instantly took away all my sadness replacing it with a peaceful sense of total forgiveness. Without His justice all would be lost. I could see the intense fiery furnace that was necessary for the punishment of sin and oh, how glad I was and the tears ceased and overwhelming peace enveloped me with grace, favor and blessings. I now understand why He allowed me to come and to return with this great urgency welled up within me. With confirmation, I am purposed to develop kingdom warriors, skillful, anointed with the fight of faith. With full authority, influence and power as Christians, we need to prepare ourselves to GO OUT as dependable, caring followers, full of godly wisdom, and focusing on His glory.

As I was pleading and asking for another chance to return to tell others, I was hearing the sounds of many voices. Some were voices from my past. It was a reverberating sound of many voices all sounding as one voice. Like rushing waters crashing against stone walls and then spreading out everywhere. I knew immediately I wanted to be one with the voices I heard, a messenger so to speak. I also realized that I had previously asked to be a messenger for this generation. And as His disciples, that is exactly what He is asking of us. Continuously try to see the world through His eyes and become a part of this great harvest that lies before us. But before we can begin, we must actively seek His attributes in order to successfully be messengers, messengers of His Glory.

I also experienced a soul and spirit separation as I stood at the Judgment Seat and before 'THE WORD'. God knew my motives were pure in asking for another chance. As I stood there my desire to tell others intensified. Everyone needed to know that the rapture was real, the judgment seat for believers is real, salvation is real! He is truly the living WORD. In His vast ability to examine my life, He proved his quickness and power. For as my life continued to pass before me as a digital picture frame, each segment carefully examined, it was showing that I was capable of being this messenger. I had asked and unbeknownst to me I first needed to endure judgment.

It was so powerful yet all I felt was nothing but meekness, unworthiness and insurmountable inadequacies. But as a result, I have been given a powerful anointing to speak with authority that which was given to me by the very authorities of heaven itself. All of this is only because of His faithfulness and absolutely nothing to do with me. Oh how, I began to feel His overpowering presence filling me with a message of declaration to His Church. I knew for certain that the WORD that had became flesh, would soon dwell amongst us. He is coming!

It was glorious being in His presence and I knew immediately that all he wanted for His radiant BRIDE was for His glorious awesome presence to be in and upon her. He wanted His BRIDE ready in full greatness, power and authority, and to be within her revealing and imparting His manifested glory with demonstrations of His many attributes through signs, wonders and miracles.

When I finally came through and returned from this most glorious encounter in the wonderful presence of God, my hair had turned white, very white. I also felt His glory all around and upon me. To this day, His glorious presence is in and upon my life. When we allow His glory to be revealed to us. We too, like Moses will eventual have to unveil ourselves and seek Him face to face. Let Him reveal his person, His wonderful presence to you. THE CHRIST IN US IS THE HOPE OF GLORY ...AMEN.

Later on in this vision I also recalled giving birth, three times to be exact. I physically experienced intense and extreme labor pains during three deliveries. The open vision continues to unfold even to this day, as I recall the things shown to me. I still don't understand all of the vision, but a lot of it is much clearer now. After twenty years of silence I am able to share many of the things foretold and the things that are happening today.

My mother did finally make it to North Carolina. It took her about four days to get to me and she moved me to Mercy Hospital in Miami, were she was employed. She had one of the doctors call to release me into his care. This doctor was the Chief of Neurology at Mercy Hospital. Here I stayed in a private room for two and a half months where I continued to live out this vision in the new heaven and the new earth.

During the vision, I witnessed the gospel being preached around the world to every nation, tribe and tongue. I saw worship in some congregations go to a level where the glory of the Lord was as thick as a cloud. God's presence was seen everywhere and in everything. There was peace like none other and the praise and worship I experienced was awesome. I also spent time writing many songs and singing them to the Lord.

On one particular day I was singing a song that I wrote, "You are precious to me, oh so precious". As I started to sing the second verse a nun walked into my hospital room. She sat down next to me and joined me. Together we continued to sing "you are lovely to me, oh so lovely to me". Praise and worship was not so popular back then as it is today. But what a blessing, I had become a praise and worshiper.

God's word tells us that everything in heaven and earth was created to worship Him. I believe my worship jumped to another level because of what I experienced in Heaven, all day long. If you are presently uncomfortable with worship, with raising your hands or humbly bowing before Him, this will change when you do get to Heaven! So why not start now.

At Mercy Hospital, I started asking for literature on the medications they were giving me. Upon learning the many disturbing side effects, including sterility, I began refusing my medications. The withdrawal from these medications caused me to draw up in a fetal position for about two days. My breasts became engorged with breast milk and I remember the doctor ordering me a breast pump. It wasn't until later that I understood the significance of this and I will share about it later in the conclusion.

In the vision, after experiencing heaven and the Judgment Throne, I returned to "The New Earth". There is an unexplainable peace on the New Earth. No crime, hate or harsh words existed. Only LOVE, and it was being shown in many different ways. I also noticed that everything around me was new. I had come back with Christ to the most peaceful place ever, and every day was like Sunday. And for the first time in my life I had unexplainable and blissful rest. But the most overwhelming thing I remember was a peace so profound. I never experienced any of the Tribulation, only the peace. And all I wanted to do was to remain right where I was. I wanted to be like Mary in Jesus' presence, sitting at His feet. It was so over whelming, I was in the presence of the Prince of Peace. Why in the world would I want to return?

I finally came home from the hospital two and a half months later. When I did, I was unable to speak but a few words to anyone for almost two years. When I look back in retrospect, I believe the only one that had the slightest idea what really happened to me, that it was not a nervous breakdown, was my father. He had spent so many days in the hospital room with me praying and listening as I would share my many experiences during the vision. I also wrote, and boy did I write. By evidence of all the completed notebooks I still have to this day, I must have emptied out many ink pens.

The doctors sent me home with so many medications. One of them caused me to sleep for days at a time. I would only wake up for meals and go right back to sleep. During this long slumber I went from a size 10 to size 26.

During this time my sister was having some difficulty sleeping so she experimented with my meds. She took just one of my pills and could not wake up for two days. I can remember her telling my mom with excitement that she discovered what was wrong with me. She kept repeating, "I know what's wrong with Carolyn, I know what's wrong with Carolyn." She showed mom the little orange pill I was taking. She had only taken one and here I was taking these as prescribed. No wonder I couldn't stay awake.

It was way out of character for me to sleep that much. Sleep had always been a problem for me most of my young adult life. I would go all week without it and usually end up crashing on Fridays. If I slept for ten hours a week, that was a good week. Insomnia is very maddening. I often would stay up all night, cleaning cracks in the floor, washing the walls and base boards, rearranging the closets and cabinets, organizing and color coding everything by size. If I wasn't cleaning or organizing, I would be reading. It wasn't uncommon to read a whole novel in one night and get up the next morning and go to work.

I experienced this vision during the "Eighties". It is important to understand that I was actually seeing things in the future. It wasn't until twenty years later that I could finally share and understand the many things I saw and heard back then. The details continue to unfold, but it wasn't until the malpractice trial that I began to recall a lot of it with clarity. His presence was right there with me and throughout the whole process God helped sustain and strengthen me. He allowed me to reopen the vision and to understand many of the details. The vision came alive again. My God is so good.

When I see and hear things as they happen twenty years later, I am so humbled by what God can do and has done. I clearly remember when He taught me about the significance and meaning of numbering and assigning numbers to the alphabet during the vision. So when I read an article about new discoveries dealings with Hebraic scriptures and numbers, it made perfect sense to me. Here was something I learned about more than twenty years earlier from the vision. God's ways are not our ways. All I can do is humbly stand in awe of the Holy presence of God as He reveals the things I saw twenty years in advance.

God had so many lessons for me to learn. But to the rest of the world, it looked like I was having a 'Nervous Breakdown'. In my heart I knew that what I experienced was real, but the rest of the world was questioning it. It took a spiritually grounded friend to help me understand that a nervous breakdown is anything but peaceful. As I was sharing with her my writings, some of the details in the vision and describing just how peaceful Christ's reign on earth was like, she strongly corrected me. "Carolyn, a nervous breakdown is anything but peaceful!" Here I was questioning the things God had revealed to me and reducing them down to a nervous breakdown. I now know it is Christ's presence that takes us through the veil.

I continue to experience true fellowship with God as He continues to lead me with the things of the future. When we don't lift Christ up as we're going through the desert wandering, it is during these times in our lives that we are in rebellion; going round and round the same mountain of deceit and unbelief in acts of defiance. But how else can we or others ever experience His presence and believe. If Christ is not lifted up, who will believe in Him and have the opportunity to receive eternal life. With all my heart I want to live with Him in the new earth, the one He showed to me.

"If I have told you earthly things and you do not believe, how will you believe if I tell you heavenly things? No one has ascended to heaven but He who came down from heaven, that is, the Son of Man who is in heaven. And as Moses lifted

up the serpent in the wilderness, even so must the Son of Man be lifted up; that whoever believes in him should not perish but have eternal life. For God so loved the world that He gave His only begotten Son, that whoever believe in Him should not perish but have everlasting life." (John 3: 12-16)

In John 3, Jesus is speaking to Nicodemus after answering him concerning being born again. If you are reading this book and have not accepted Jesus as your Lord and Savior, I extend the invitation to you right now. Jesus said to Nicodemus: *"Most assuredly, I say to you, unless one is born again, he cannot see the kingdom of God."*

I gave my heart to Jesus at the age of 12, at a revival in my Father's church in Lake Placid, Florida. I had spent a week in Lake Placid with my father and my mom stayed in Miami because she had to work. When I returned, I remember being so excited about getting ready for the next school year to start. I also wanted to go outside to play with my friends and to share with them what a wonderful summer I had. My Father however wanted me to tell my Mom about giving my heart to Jesus. All I wanted to do was to go and play, so I said to her, "if you tell someone about it they will take it away", and out the door I went to play. What childish thoughts.

Can you imagine my parents laughing? So is heaven rejoicing when just one lost soul comes to know Jesus and is born again. I received my 'Born Again' experience at Shaw University. Rev. C. T. Vivian was preaching one night and I was singing in the gospel choir. I began shouting to the Lord with dance and I continued to do so right out the Chapel door and all over Shaw's Campus. And those that know me today know that I'm still shouting and dancing.

I gave my heart to God at age 12 but I was not born again until age 19. Is there a difference between the two experiences? It is my belief there is a difference. Jesus told Nicodemus, *"that which is born of flesh is flesh, and that which is born of the Spirit is spirit."* At age 12, I gave Jesus my heart, but I didn't accept Him into my heart until later. There lies the difference. The Bible says: *"that if you confess with your mouth the LORD JESUS and BELIEVE in your heart that God has raised Him from the dead, you will be saved. For with the heart one believes unto righteousness, and with the mouth confession is made unto salvation."* *(Romans 10:9)*

I feel we have many members in our churches that are in the same shape I was in. In my born again experience everything looked new. Even my hands and my feet looked different. If this is you and you have given Jesus your heart, but have not invited Him into your heart to be Lord of your life, pray this prayer with me:

Dear Heavenly Father,

I confess that I am a sinner and I need a Savior to deliver me. I ask forgiveness for all my sins and thank you that I did not die in them. Please forgive me my sins for they are many, and I'm so sorry. Father, I believe that you sent your Son to die so that my sins may be forgiven, I believe He was crucified, buried and resurrected that I might have eternal life. I accept what you have done for me, Jesus, and I ask that you please come into my heart. I'm grateful for you Lord Jesus Christ. Please come into my heart and be Lord over me, all of me. Thank You. AMEN.

If you prayed this prayer let me congratulate you and welcome you into the family of God. Now, if you do not have other believers to fellowship with regularly, find yourself a bible teaching church. Now, look at your hands and see if they look new. Just kidding, but mine did and others say that their hands and their feet did too. Get connected and stay hooked up to the vine. Jesus said: *"I am the true vine, and My Father is the vine dresser."*

I did get hooked up to the vine, I abide in His presence. Do you remember when I told you earlier that I had three births in the vision and that I did not know what it meant. Well, God knows everything. He is omniscient and all wise and knows how to lead us beside the still waters. Miami is where I got hooked up to the vine with my mother's prompting. She said to me, "Carolyn you must get back into the church and train your daughter, Buttons, in the way."

I listened to what my mother said and I walked down the street to a church in my neighborhood and started attending with Buttons. I'm not going to tell you it was easy to sit through a service. Because of all the medications I was on, my attention span was so short. Every time they would sing or do something different, I would get the urge to leave. This would happen right after any song or after the collection of the offering. This went on for a period of time until I finally got to the place where I wanted nothing else but to be there where God was.

I continued to grow closer to God after staying in the church and abiding in him. Then, a few years later came hurricane Andrew. Due to all the damage this hurricane caused to our home, we had to leave our neighborhood and my church. I found myself wandering around through a sea of self pity. It was during this time that my Mom passed away. To top it all, my Dad remarried less than a year after her death. My mom was my best friend. I had never allowed others to get close enough to me because of my fear of rejection. But I was very glad I was in Miami with my family and that God had led me here. I now had Gwen, my big sis, to help me with decision making.

My younger sister, Marilyn, was still living in North Carolina and I missed her very much. We lived together most of our lives and raised our children together. And when her marriage failed, she also came home to Miami and lived with us until she eventually remarried. Since I never allowed others outside of my family to become close to me, having both of my sisters with me was very comforting. I continued to do well, and eventually I went back to teaching.

God lead me to Miami, to the place where I discovered the significance of abiding in His presence and to begin my journey in becoming a true disciple, a follower of Jesus Christ. When His grace abounds everywhere and in everything you do, you can see His leading evident in your surrender.

His Presence

Comforts Us

I have battled with obesity my entire life. I won some of the battles, but I also lost many, including the gastric bypass surgery that almost cost me my life. The lawsuit took several years and in the meantime, my primary doctor deemed me to be severely depressed and he prescribed medications. To make matters worse, I also saw a psychiatrist and of course, he also prescribed an additional medication for depression.

I'd lost 180 pounds and almost died in the process. And now these doctors where prescribing medications that caused weight gain. I ended up going from a size 4 to a size 16. Mind you, I never really got to enjoy the size 4 because of the time it took me to recuperate from the botched surgery. Again, I found myself crying out to the Lord asking the

Father to please help me. I was so tired of battling the weight fluctuations like a yo-yo. You will never guess who God sent to help me.

Before I share with you who God sent, let me tell you something about depression. It is a condition that robs you of your very essence of being. My last bout with depression, and I mean my last, was the worst ever. This time it became crippling and I could not even go out of the house. All I could do was wallow in self pity. Nothing anyone tried to do for me would help or make it go away. I didn't bathe for weeks at a time. I stopped all fellowship at church and I refused all calls. Lost in a world of despair, I did not see how God could even help someone like me.

It was, without a doubt, the lowest point of my life. My body was so maimed and disfigured from the massive weight loss, it was hard to look into the mirror. My breasts sagged almost to my waist, my thighs were so wrinkled they looked like a bucket of chitlings. And because of the loose skin, every time I moved my arms they flapped. I started calling them chicken wings and began to inquire about corrective surgery to eliminate this burden of flesh. My doctor at the time adamantly advised me not to have corrective surgery any time soon.

Feeling trapped in a body that was ugly; I had lost weight but was ashamed to look at myself in the mirror. How was I ever to get married looking like this? I experienced some of the darkest hours spent in my life left without hope. Having no desire to continue living, I fell into total darkness and my depression spiraled out of control. Stopping all medication and shutting off the world, I thought I could never recover.

During this terrible time of despair, my niece Antralyn and her little girl named Ambralyn came to live with us. I recall a strange experience while Ambralyn was still in her mother's womb. We were at a yard sale and a lady searching for treasures commented on my niece's pregnancy and she asked if Antralyn was having twins. The lady actually drove off but was strongly compelled to return. When she returned she began to give us a word of knowledge and told us that someday the Lord would use Ambralyn mightily.

Remember when I mentioned that you would be surprised who God would send to help me. Every morning I would go get little Ambralyn and take her in my arms and sing, *"This is the day the Lord has made, I will rejoice and be glad in it"*. Not realizing the power of words, it didn't take long of repeating this routine, that I realized the depression was all gone. During this time of hopelessness, I had lost my focus and my foundation. My rock was on sinking sand. But now I was looking to the source of all comfort, Almighty God, my El Shaddai. He is my mighty unconquerable mountain, which is His greatness and my strength. And in His everlasting nature He becomes my all sufficient God and is eternally capable of being all that I need.

With this experience and God's presence, I was being challenged to return to my spiritual roots. All I ever have known was the Lord crucified for me, buried and raised on the third day morn, raised just like my blessed hope was raised and renewed. I cried out, "God comfort me like none other, please." I begged the Lord to return to me the joy of my salvation and He did.

While reading the bible He showed me *(Isaiah 51: 3)* *"For the Lord will comfort Zion, He will comfort all her waste places; He will make her wilderness like Eden, And her desert like the garden of the Lord; Joy and gladness will be found in it, thanksgiving and the voice of melody."* Pure fellowship with the Almighty God is all I desired, my Eden.

In this new found comfort of abiding in His Presence, my desire to walk closely with Him became an obsession. I have previously experienced His Presence as I sang a melody of love songs to Him while driving all the way from Raleigh,

NC to Miami, FL. Without the aid of radio, tapes or CDs, it was a glorious time of nonstop praise and worship for about sixteen hours. Now I can't imagine anything better than to be taken up with Him eternally and to remain in His presence singing love songs of praise all the day long.

I now know that happiness is a choice, just like being depressed all those years was also my choice. We make our choice to be happy and sad. I remember reading this in Joel Osteen's book; 'Living Your Best Life Now.' And I can see how, for years, food was my escape from reality. I wandered through years of depression feeding on my sorrow. I was without an excuse just like it will be in the day of recompense. We will all be without an excuse. And God keeps telling me to tell His people; He wants to comfort you, He wants to give you a future and a hope.

"The wilderness and the wasteland shall be glad for them, And the desert shall rejoice and blossom abundantly and rejoice, Even with joy and singing, The glory of Lebanon shall be given to it, the excellence of Carmel, and Sharon, they shall see the glory of the Lord, The excellence of our God. Strengthen the weak hands and make firm the feeble knees. Say to those who are fearful-hearted, Be strong,

do not fear! Behold, your God will come with vengeance, with the recompense of God; He will come and save you." With the recompense of God; He will come and save you." Then the eyes of the blind shall be opened, And the ears of the deaf shall be unstopped. Then the lame shall leap like a deer, and the tongue of the dumb sing. For waters shall burst forth in the wilderness, And streams in the desert. The parched ground shall become a pool, and the thirsty land springs of water; In the habitation of jackals where each lay, There shall be grass with reeds and rushes. A highway shall be there, and a road and it shall be called the Highway of Holiness. The unclean shall pass over it, but it shall be for others. Whoever walks the road, although a fool shall not go astray. No lion shall be there. But the redeemed shall walk there, and the ransomed of the Lord shall return and come to Zion singing with everlasting joy on their heads. They shall obtain joy and gladness, and sorrow and sighing shall flee away." (Isaiah 35:1-10)

Yes, we all have hope. Walk on in spite of all your heart's down cast moments, all infirmities, transgressions, judgments and sin. It is necessary to pick yourself up and walk with your El Shaddai on the Highway of Holiness. He gave us righteousness by justification through Christ. Throughout the prophets like Isaiah, God still sends the message of restoration in spite of our sin and judgment. Just as I stood at the judgment seat saying, "Lord please give me another chance", so will you be, without excuse.

Let Him comfort you by restoring you to your rightful place in Him. The Highway of Holiness is one of joy and gladness. No matter what you have been through in life, whether it's the hard times or the good times, just know in your heart that now is the time to get right. Like Lisa Kemp puts it in her song, "Get Right or Get Left." And know that all of God's blessings to Israel are our promises too. *"And as many as walk according to this rule, peace and mercy be upon them and upon the Israel of God." (Galatians 6:16)*

With all that I am, I believe God allowed me to live this open vision to help prepare His bride, the church, for His return. During the vision I previously told you about three births. I did not understand these at the time. However, the vision came to past with the birth of triplets; Izavahlyn Deyan, Imyahlyn Denae and Inyahlyn Denene, all born on May 16, 2009 to my daughter Iris, YES Buttons! My precious Lord gave to me, three adorable grand- daughters all natural, no in-vitro fertilization. My daughter had been told she could not have children, but my God is a God of miracles.

For thirteen years, my daughter Iris was suffering from postpartum depression but we didn't know it. She had driven everyone away from her, including all her relatives and friends. I prayed long and hard for my daughter to come back. She was very different, no one recognized Buttons any more. This was a person full of rage and anger and our relationship became estranged, I had lost my only child. But now, Praise God, for all had been restored.

As soon as my daughter found out she was pregnant, the symptoms she was suffering from disappeared, and restoration and healing began. While she was pregnant with the triplets, God was a comfort to both of us. Countless times during the pregnancy, God reminded me of many details in the open vision. He also gave Iris assurance that severed relationships would be restored through a dream she had of her babies wearing diapers and building bridges.

After the babies were born, Iris told me that God had answered her prayers. He had given her back the daughter she lost at age 19. This baby was an eight month old still borne. Our God is truly the God of all comfort. The daughter

I had lost was returned to me in full fellowship with God and my bonus was three beautiful granddaughters.

In fellowship with God's promise, I know I will see the rapture. But I still have promises to keep and that is to tell everyone I know, He is coming soon. I received a written prophesy that said: "Carolyn, I want you to take note that there are some things and areas in your life where you are going to begin to experience the blessings of the Lord that maketh rich and adds no sorrow."

I also heard the word of the Lord saying: "that as you are moving forward in life, you are a messenger, like 'John the Baptist' that has come to prepare the way of salvation. You have been unaware of how important your mission is, unwilling to take the time or the trouble to develop your intuition, which is your greatest gift. You are an individual that operates on another level spiritually. You are a bearer of the light for those that are still stuck in the threshold of light. Yet you are called to help them to come into the awareness of who they are and what they are given to do."

After receiving this prophesy I posted it on the wall in my bedroom, where I often post words of prophecy. I've gone to every one of my family members and have asked them what would the rapture find them doing. I have also asked them if they are ready. The following prayer was added to the top of my prophesy's: "Father I ask you to position me in your harvest, thank you that you will. " I needed to do this to continue to remind myself that God has a specific purpose and plan for me, and He has one for you too.

God gently and continuously reminds me that the open vision is real. The birth of the triplets confirmed that He has fulfilled what He had shown me twenty-three years in advance. He still continues confirming the open vision as He reminds me of things that were said.

At the birth of the babies, I clearly heard Him say to me; "When you were in the hospital, yes Mercy Hospital, did you not have breast milk after giving birth in the vision. The doctor ordered a breast pump and the nurses began to laugh saying; "don't you know that produces more milk?"

I'm the one laughing now, because no one can make me doubt that Jesus is not on His way back. However, this will not happen until "We", those that are faithful and believe, receive our reward, THE RAPTURE! Even greater rewards will we receive in eternity.

I have written this book to tell all of God's creation to get ready. Are you ready? Everything God has created is created to return back to Him. If you do not know what you need to do to get ready for this blessed hope, the answer is simple; claim His presence in your life. Yes that's right, ask the Father to help you walk in His presence. There is safety when we abide in the presence of God. *"He who dwells in the secret place of the Most High God shall abide under the shadow of the Almighty." (Psalm 91)*

That's what He has created us to do. Nothing can please the Father more than for all of us to be saved and to abide in His presence. Do you know that God created us for His pleasure? Our loving, caring and forgiving Father is waiting to comfort each and every one of us. It does not matter what life roads you've traveled. At the end of the journey and all along the way, if you remain faithful, you will be comforted abundantly.

Abiding in
His Presence

Every time the children of Israel would put their trust in anything other than God or turn their hearts away from God, calamity occurred in their lives. Often times God would remove Himself from them because they took His presence for granted.

There have been so many times God has intervened in my life. It wasn't until lately that I learned the importance of guarding His presence. Once I recognized the fullness of His presence in my life, I tried exceptionally hard never to take it for granted and I made sure to guard it with all my heart.

You have heard of the term "stiff-necked and uncircumcised." In the Old Testament, this related to sins against the Holy Spirit; God's presence among them. Many times we bring harm to ourselves by offending the person of the Holy Spirit.

As I realized and accepted the realty of the Holy Spirit and how He wants and desires for me to remain in fellowship with Him, my life began to change dramatically. This increasing reality became a hunger to start looking more into the Word of God not only for comfort but for instruction. To embrace the warmness of the Holy Spirit was my obsession. I did not ever want to offend Him or cause Him to decrease, I only wanted more and more. As each of us draw closer to Him His word declares He will draw closer to us and that's exactly what happened.

It was at the point in my life that this new instruction helped me. I was without hope and did not know how I was ever going to recover from the black hole I was in called 'depression'. So, with that said, I want to share with you what the New Testament says about the five ways our friend and constant companion, the Holy Spirit, can be offended:

1. Blaspheme against the Holy Spirit. This is the only unpardonable sin. (Mark 3: 29, 30) Blasphemy accepts as truth the lie that our LORD was filled with an unclean or even a demonic spirit, rather than filled

with the presence of God. Such a position is a dangerous position to be in because it denies that Jesus is the Son of God. If anyone continues or persists in this attitude unrepentant until death, it is unpardonable.

2. Grieve the Holy Spirit (Ephesians 4:30, 31). Paul here made it plain that we can grieve the Spirit with whom you are sealed for the day of redemption. Let me make this plain to you. If I allow and believe the lie that the Lord is not powerful enough to accomplish what He declared, and that is to keep me whole; body, spirit and soul, then the name 'depression' or whatever your black hole is will become greater than the name of Jesus whose name is above all names.

3. Despise the Holy Spirit (I Thessalonians 4:8). In this offense we clearly set aside what God's moral law and will is. We are being defiant (stiff-necked and uncircumcised). We, by our own action and our intentions, declare invalid what God has declared to be valid.

4. Quench the Spirit (I Thessalonians 5:19). This has to do with extinguishing and snuffing the move of the Holy Spirit. If we look at Matthew 12:20, we can infer that we sometimes disregard (spiritually) the prompting's of the Holy Spirit. We quench His

Spirit of compassion and mercy by failing to fully be directed by Him.

5. Resist the Holy Spirit. *"Ye stiff-necked and uncircumcised in heart and ears, ye do always resist the Holy Ghost; as your fathers did, so do ye." (Acts 7:51)* Rejecting truth is the point of all the offenses. Obedience and walking by faith are signs of a true relationship. Anything else indicates a Spirit of rebellion.

I know that all that I am and all that I hope to be are in the one who created me for his Glory. [Revelation 4:11] One day I will be in His presence forever singing, alleluia to the Lamb of God, never to be separated, Amen. The lesson above on the offenses of the Holy Spirit was shared in hopes that you will draw near to Him and hunger for a closer relationship that will dramatically affect your life. Once you recognize these truths, you will find yourself communicating on all levels with the third person of the Trinity, the Holy Spirit.

I will never forget the lessons I had to learn on abiding and letting God take up residence within me. The importance of these teachings are significant, especially to understand them. They let you actualize who you are abiding in, the true vine.

Each and every day, I will praise the Lord for He abides with me as I abide with him. I thank you My Teacher, Oh Holy Spirit, for today and every day.

TODAY

As it is called Today, I will rejoice and be glad.
For my future is in your hand.

As it is called Today, I will offer thanksgiving and be full.
For my destiny is etched in the palm of your hand.

As it is call Today, I will praise you and be complete.
For all is yours, even me LORD. Even me.

I truly know without a doubt that His work was complete and that His desire for me is to be perfect. So I wrote the previous poem to express to him that my life journey has not been wasted. As long as it is called today, I will continue to acknowledge His presence and to accomplish in obedience, all He created me to be. My destiny is truly etched in the scars of His hands, signifying my wholeness. Jesus made me whole.

Prior to the malpractice trial, I had experienced three rear-enders. These car accidents left me with a herniated disk in my neck and some pain radiating down my left arm. So, here I found myself, fearful of driving and in pain. I needed to resist this fear, so I began by quoting the word of the Lord; *"Perfect love cast out all fear"* and *"no weapon formed against me shall prosper."*

During this time, a minister from India had come to visit at our church. That night I could feel the pain radiating down my left arm as a result of the previous car accidents. While Brother Rajan from Heart International Ministries was preaching, I kept quoting the word of the Lord, *"Perfect love cast out all fear"* and *"no weapon formed against me shall prosper."* That night the presence of God was overwhelming. Not only was I healed of all pain, but also of my fear. And I was left with a compelling desire to go to India.

Brother Rajan preached on a Friday night. The next day we had 'Prayer Mountain', which is a corporate prayer meeting held every first Saturday of the Month at my church. During this meeting I prayed for confirmation from God that He was calling me to India. When this prayer meeting was finished, two other ladies and I went out to lunch. On the way to the restaurant, one of the ladies began to speak of a mission trip.

Wouldn't you know it, she and Brother Rajan were planning a mission trip, and guess where, to India! This sister happened to be a facilitator at my church for one of the classes at Global University Study Center. She taught History and Missions. As it happens, she was inquiring about a mission trip for her class. Even though I wasn't a student of her class at the time, this mission trip was to be extended to all the Global University students. I qualified. Talk about someone praising God! That was my sign, Hallelujah. Brother Rajan returned to India and shortly after he began to organize this mission trip and the trip became official.

I wish I could tell you everything went smoothly from that point on. I had said YES to God, but the devil said, oh, no. This was the beginning of the most important lesson I will ever need to learn. I had to learn to totally abide in God; to put my trust in no one else, especially not man. And, I needed to learn to recognize how God prunes us so that we may bear much fruit. There was a lot of cutting away; of self, of others, along with the battle of my own will.

When one answers God's call, opposition usually begins. Initially I wasn't taken seriously about the trip. I had to convince others that God was calling me to India. Circumstances caused me to wait a long time before I was given an appointment to meet with the Pastor in charge of missions. It was only after he saw and felt my persistence, along with my determination, did he finally approve my participation. Yes, there were concerns, regarding my health, but I convinced everyone I was well. Permission was granted, fund raising began. Opposition continued to challenge me up until the ninth hour.

Since I had started the process so late, all the other members of the mission team had already distributed their request letters to the congregation. These letters were given to the other members of the church for prayer and financial support. In the middle of all that was going on, there was God, teaching me to abide in only Him.

Dying to self was my first lesson. I wanted things to go as I planned them, but our ways are not God's ways, neither are our thoughts. I chose to walk in disappointment because I had lost so much time getting out my letters to the congregation. But again, God spoke out. He said, "I did not tell you to go to the congregation for donations." Did you notice the word…I? The great I AM told me to get out of His way. Now that's what I call, dying to self. Get rid of what you want. He is your Shepherd and you shall not want. You were bought with a price and it's a much bigger "I" that lives. Christ lives within you. My God supernaturally touched family, friends and community. The funds to finance this trip came from many different sources; however, the greatest challenge was still to come.

It was July 17, I came home from volunteering at the church for eight hours and I had a vomiting episode which is common with gastric bypass surgery. My blood pressure had shot up to 270 over 142 and I passed out. My daughter Iris heard me hit the floor with a loud thump and I thank God, because I was unconscious and still vomiting. She immediately called 911 and they gave her instructions until the paramedics arrived.

My, oh my, what was I to do now? Give back all the money raised, or believe in the promise of the Lord... that I was already healed. The mission trip was scheduled for September 17-27. When I got to the emergency room they explained that I had a brain hemorrhage and I needed to be transported by ambulance to another hospital in case surgery was necessary. Through all of this, God's presence was with me. He sent me to another hospital accompanied by a nurse from the first hospital in the ambulance.

I arrived at the other hospital to an overcrowded and backed-up emergency waiting room. This hospital was known for always being chaotic and overcrowded. My sister had once spent two days in the hallway of this emergency room and that is exactly where they were going to put me. However, the nurse that had ridden with me in the ambulance, the one from the other hospital, demanded that they monitor my blood pressure and vitals closely. They immediately assigned me to a room.

All the doctors and staff that were working with me kept telling me how lucky I was. And I would reply, "NO, Blessed." I knew no luck was in this. In addition, my niece, who is an RN, was given authority by the attending doctor, to see the x-rays of the hemorrhage, she was able to verify all that they were saying. At one point she came into the room with tears in her eyes, saying, "Auntie, you are truly blessed. Because of the location and the amount of the bleeding, you should have deficits." Deficits are impairments in speech, hearing, motor skills and even paralysis, and here I was with nothing. God had healed me supernaturally from this massive stroke. The only active residue I had was to convince everyone that my trip to India, which was less than a month and a half away, was still on.

Physical therapists were assigned to come to my house to work with me. I explained the urgency I had to recuperate quickly so that I could go on this mission trip to India. They both said it was possible if I worked hard enough. I was asked what I normally did for exercise and that's where we started. First we walked with the walker, then with a cane, and finally full throttle. It wasn't long before they had me back outside doing early morning 'prayer walks' and praying for my community. What I later realized was that it also prepared me for all the walking I would be doing throughout the mission trip.

I had many concerns since this was my first mission trip abroad. But I knew God was calling me to India, so I stood firm on His words and trusted in Him alone. In spite of all the opposition, He brought it to pass. *"No weapon formed against me prospered and every tongue that rose in judgment was condemned, this was my heritage as his servant and my righteousness was from him and He did speak."* *[Isaiah 54:17]* God kept me whole, spiritually, physically and mentally.

It would be an understatement to say God was pruning me, cutting away my will, and delivering me from others. On the Friday before our mission trip, around 11:00 AM, I was asked to obtain a medical clearance note from the doctor. That Friday happened to be a Jewish Holy Day. But our God is faithful; I had not just one, but two doctor's notes, one from my primary physician and one from the neurologist saying I was physically able to go on this trip. To God Be the Glory!

On that same night before the trip, I received another phone call demanding to know why I wasn't in church. The mission team leaving for India had been prayed over by the pastors and congregation and I was not there. God's all abiding presence spoke and said to me "be quiet". And when His presence prompted me to speak, I said, "I was making preparation for the trip to India." The person on the phone said, "Oh," and just hung up. If I had mentioned the word doctor or doctor's note, I strongly believe that I would not have gone on that trip. The reason I wasn't in church was because I was still in the doctor's office getting the ninth hour medical clearance. The enemy was working overtime to stop me.

I was later told that the church would absorb the costs and they didn't expect me to raise all of the funds needed for the trip. All I can say is that when you abide in Him and Him in you, it pleases the Father. I was putting my trust in God who was calling me to India and not in man. Not only did I have the medical clearance notes, but God had miraculously provided all the monies. One of the first contribution checks was for $500 dollars. I noticed that the amount donated had been changed from $200 dollars to $500 dollars. Later the contributor told me that a voice had spoken to him and said, "You can do better than that." Here again, God extends His ability to let me know He is always with me.

On the Sunday of our departure, around three o'clock in the afternoon, God again reassured me I would be safe and that He was going with me. I continued to stay in prayer, concerned about the possible affects the high altitudes might have on the brain hemorrhage.

At three o'clock the Sunday before we left, I went to lunch with someone who is well known for prophesy. As we were having our lunch, a couple I had never seen before walked in and sat down at the table next to us. All of a sudden the prophetess turned to the couple and said directly to the woman, "Do you have something to say to someone here?" She looked embarrassed and hesitant, but she turned to me and said: "The Lord wants you to know it's going to be well with you in India and that He is with you." On hearing this, I was blown away. I had never seen this lady before and as far as I know, she knew nothing of my trip to India. God had given her this word, just for me.

When we arrived in London the next day, I could tell something was wrong with my legs. Our mission team had several health care professionals with us. I could not let them know that I had developed blood clots in my legs during the flight from Miami to London. Upon arrival in India, I stood firm on the word God had given to me at the restaurant by a total stranger. Staying in continuous prayer I decided to tell my roommate what was going on. I begged her not to tell anyone and together we prayed and came into agreement.

Each evening after we returned from the villages, I would place my suitcase at the foot of the bed and prop up my feet and legs. My roommate would bring me warm wash cloths and lay them across my legs. That's how I slept and the next morning the swelling was down. I wore long skirts and no one noticed the redness in my legs. I did not even go to the doctor for the clots when I returned to Miami. It went well with me personally in India and God was with all of us. He demonstrated His power through miracles, signs, and wonders.

This was an exciting time in my life. I now can truly identify with David's walk in faith. By accepting the call to

India, I experienced a personal journey that fulfilled my trust in God, my trust in the Word and what the Bible teaches, and most importantly, my trust in His character. This mission trip was a divine journey into understanding God's anointing on my life as a complete faith walk believer.

God's awesome presence is so wonderful; especially when you realize the extent He will go in order to let you know He is there. Greater works than Jesus we are able to do when we abide in Him. We witnessed people who were deaf, receive hearing; others who were mute, speak; people who were lame, walk. We also witnessed many other diseases healed and souls saved! What an amazing honor to serve the Lord. I had personally learned and received the single most important lesson of my life. I realized the significance of abiding in Him and how my future can and will be affected when I do not.

"Most assuredly, I say to you, he who believes in me, the works that I do he will do also; and greater works than these he will do, because I go to My Father, and whatever you ask in My name, that I will do, that the Father may be glorified in the Son. If you ask anything in my name, I will do it." (John 14: 12-14)

God spoke and told me to meditate on that particular scripture. The lesson He wanted me to learn concerns meditating on His Word. When I begin to read or study the Bible, I also need to meditate on it because there is more. God is teaching us that man shall not live by bread alone, but by every word that proceeds out of the mouth of God. The greater works God speaks of includes temptations, trials and opposition just like Jesus himself endured. His primary desire is for us to remain available to Him and His word. Not sometimes, but all the time. He does not call us to produce more, but to ask and believe in Him for the greater works, all to advance His Kingdom, purpose and glory.

I learned the essence of abiding in the vine during the initial part of this trip. My life had changed dramatically and I fully recognized that I move and have my being because of Him. The very breath that I breathe is because of Him and my total trust in Him is what sustains my life. Trust is the key word in abiding in Him. See, God tests us to see what our faith is made of. Is yours that of sight or are you walking in faith?

As Abraham's faith was tested, and so will ours, Abraham purposed in his heart to be obedient. And like Abraham, obedience should be our response to faith, especially to the word of God. The word of God says, *"All the nations of the earth shall be blessed because Abraham obeyed my voice and kept my charge, my commandments, my statues and my laws."* *(Genesis 26: 4-5)*

I know God was calling me to serve in India but my trust was in every source but the one who was calling me. When we are abiding in Him, we can't allow our loyalties to be divided. All the offenses I endured leading up to the trip were a test of my faith. God wanted me to learn His word concerning trust, and this trust only comes by abiding in Him. I needed to learn this lesson and I did while I was in India.

Our mission team committed to come alongside the 'Dunamis School of Ministry' to sponsor a crusade. All the banners and posters had already been distributed and a couple of hours before the crusade, as we waited in the lobby, our group received a request for prayer. The crusade had to be moved to another venue. It seems that the owner of the original field site had suddenly become afraid of retaliation.

So, we went back up stairs to pray. All of us understood the forces of the evil one. He wanted everything to fall apart. However, we stood firm on His word and on the scripture verses He had given to us during our morning devotion.

Our trust had been united in the matchless name of Jesus. And it became magnified as we waited at that hotel room together, all in one accord, praising and praying to our God. In the meantime the students from the "Dunamis School of Ministry" and Brother Rajan were running around frantically believing God for another venue site to host this crusade. They only had a matter of hours to make it happen.

Perfect love cast out all fears I tell you. God already had us hemmed in and His holy presence had gone before us. The praise team and the ministers of the school had, within one hour, found a location and set everything up temporarily for just the first night of the crusade. They also made all announcements of the location change. God had miraculously prepared another heart to believe that all things are possible and allowed us to use their land. They also transported all the people from the original site to the new site.

While everyone was frantically moving equipment and setting up, a young woman living nearby was contemplating suicide. She had heard the praise music playing as they were testing and setting-up. This young lady came out of her home, onto the field, and immediately gave her life to Jesus. Our faithful, all knowing God had made this all possible. He changed the venue, touched the heart of another, and allowed enough time for the mission team to come together on one accord. The 'school of ministry' students were amazing and their determination to finish strong in Him was clearly evident. I watched God at work all around us as everyone involved; the school, our team and the young woman, step out in faith and trust in His lead. So, when God is leading you, trust Him, He sees the big picture, you can only see and know small parts. I will always remember this lesson of trusting in Him and not in man.

"Thus says the Lord: Cursed is the man who trusts in man and makes flesh his strength. Whose heart departs from the LORD. For he shall be like a shrub in the desert, and shall not see when good comes, But shall inhabit the parched places in the wilderness, in a salt land which is not inhabited. Blessed is the man who trusts in the LORD, and whose hope is the LORD. For he shall be like a tree planted by the waters, which spreads out its roots by the river, and will not fear when heat comes; but its leaf will be green, and will not be anxious in the year of drought, nor will cease from yielding fruit. The heart is deceitful above all things, and desperately wicked; who can know it? I, the LORD, search the heart, I test the mind, Even to give every man according

to his ways, According to the fruit of his doings." (Jeremiah 17:5-10)

Oh, I learned how important this second lesson of abiding in Him and trusting in Him is. He knows our hearts, our mind and our actions are reflective of these things. Our Lord and Savior Jesus has taught us, that what is really true faith, will always appear in our obedience to Him and in His revealed will for our lives. God's will, will be done regardless. He is sovereign.

That is why I can't emphasize enough how important it is for you to seek His will for your life. God has a purpose for each one of us. Sometimes we are out of place because we listen to every voice but the Shepherd's voice. We can wander through life on our own. However we will not have the care and protection that the loving good Shepherd provides for His fold. And without the guidance of His rod and staff, we will be out of place and will behave differently. Our true success comes from living a life of seeking and knowing what God's will is and doing it by faith.

God is searching the earth for the ones who are willing to obey and recognize that He is their Shepherd. Searching for those that will obey His voice by resting in His Redemptive

Names, those found in the Psalm of David, (Psalm 23). No good thing will He withhold from us. He wants His bride, the church, in a place of rest, knowing He is their Good Shepherd.

The Redeeming Good Shepherd, in which the confidence I now have, came from the refreshing knowledge that God has provided and completed the work of Shepherd in the work and person of Jesus Christ.

Psalm 23

The Lord is my Shepherd
(Jehovah-Rohi; the Lord my Shepherd)

I shall not want or lack
(Jehovah Jireh; God who faithfully provides)
The Resurrected Great Shepherd makes me lie down in green pasture.

He leads me beside the still and restful waters
(Jehovah-Shalom; God of Peace)

He refreshes and restores my soul
(Jehovah-Rapha; God that heals)

He leads me in the paths of righteousness for His name's sake.
(Jehovah-Tskkene; God of Righteousness)

*Yes, though I walk through the shadow of death, I will fear
or dread no evil*
(Jehovah-Makah; God who Smites)

For you, are with me. Your rod and staff they comfort me
(Jehovah-Gmolah; God of Recompense)

The returning Chief Shepherd prepares the table.

He prepares the table before me in the presence of my enemy
(Jehovah; Shammah; God of Presence)

You anoint my head with oil, my cup runs over
(Jehovah-Mikaddesh; God who Sanctifies)

*Surely goodness, mercy and unfailing love shall follow me
all the days of my life*
(Jehovah; God of Host)

And I will dwell in the house of the LORD forever.

I sought so many times to walk in the calling I thought God had for my life. As I told you earlier, I was in seminary school. I knew God had called me into the ministry at the age of 16. Like Jonah, I ran and did everything I knew to keep from answering God's call. It took me until the age of 32 to finally say YES.

I will never forget the sermon I preached after I told the Lord, YES. This sermon was titled: "Do you love me?" And after I returned home from church that night, I found an automobile that belonged to my neighbor across the street, inside my daughter's room. I shouted up and down the street, "Yes, I love you Lord and yes to your will and to your way." You see, if I had not gone to church that night, in answer to God's call, my daughter would have been sitting in front of her television on the floor right where the neighbor's car was sitting, or on her bed. The television had propelled its way across the room and had landed right on top of her bed. Either way, bed or floor, the outcome would not have been good.

From that moment I continued to say yes, but I was never certain of God's specific calling. With all my heart I wanted to know what God wanted me to do for him. And here I was under the impression that the preaching I was doing was a result of the premature advancement that had come from helping my father at such an early age.

Every door I tried to enter in the ministry was shut. Every credible opportunity became null and void. And every opening 'man' tried to advance me in, God put a halt to it. It wasn't until I took God's word and started to eat it like it was the only substance I needed, did I realize. We personally must become aware that the fruitfulness of the word is affected by our intimate response to it and by how much we are willing to be taught by it.

It wasn't until I determined in my heart to obey all of it and not just some of it, that the doors for ministry started opening for me. Remember I told you I received the call at age sixteen and answered at age thirty two. However, it wasn't until I started abiding and putting my whole trust in Him, twenty-five years later, that I finally knew my purpose and my call.

Things needed to take place. A lot of pruning, cutting away and dying to my will was necessary before this was accomplished. It is now only Him I seek to please and obey. That is what all abiding means; seeking to please Him and allowing His word to cleanse us. Jesus is the true vine we are abiding in. Paul says; *"therefore we make it our aim, whether present or absent, to be well pleasing to Him. Whether present or absent...For the love of Christ compels us, because we judge thus: if one died for all, then all died; and He died for all, that those who live should live no longer for themselves, but for Him who died for them and rose again." (2 Corinthians 5:9-15)*

Seeking to please Him is important in obeying His commandments. As Christ's love for His Father compelled him to finish in obedience what He needed to do, we also need to "sun echo" (soon-ekh-oh). Strong's dictionary defines: **sun**; together, **echo**; to hold together; or to grip tightly. There is a sense of constraint, a tight grip that prevents an escape. Jesus finished what His Father gave Him to do. Because He loved us so much, He died for us.

Paul understood this well, not only did he share the fellowship of His suffering, but also the triumph of following Jesus. As followers of Christ, we need to live lives that are godly, so that others may see we are new creations. Love is what compels us.

The pain of death was Christ's alone, but the benefit of His death is given to all with a condition, that you abide and put your trust in Him alone.

The condition of a believer is not based on works nor so called Godly living alone. It's a heart condition that is surrendered by faith in all that Christ's love accomplished for us. And that same love compels us to accomplish what we are created for, and that is to love one another unconditionally.

During my open vision when I was called up and stood before Christ at the judgment seat, I believed and thought that I had loved enough. But as my life opened up before me and I saw how little my love was, and the many areas that I failed to show Christ's love, remorse overwhelmingly over took me. All I wanted was another chance. Now I understand the importance of every action we do to others. We need to love as Christ loves us.

I have been crucified with Christ; it is no longer I who live, but Christ lives in me; and the life which I now live in the flesh I live by faith in the Son of God, who loved me and gave Himself for me." (Galatians 2:20)

"Abide in me, and I in you. As the branch cannot bear fruit of itself, unless it abides in the vine, neither can you unless you abide in me. I am the vine you are the branches, He who

abides in me, and I in him, bears much fruit; for without me you can do nothing." (John 15: 4-5)

The fruit that our heavenly vine dresser is talking about is our CHRIST LIKENESS, in which we invite the help of the Holy Spirit to enable us to produce these fruits. The adversities that come into our lives help make us mature and productive for the Kingdom of our Lord and Savior Jesus Christ. I've certainly had my share.

When we stand strong, "sun echo", we allow the fruit of the spirit in us to remain continuously present with Him. However, when we do not reject the devil's wiles, it causes us to misalign our trust, to become independent from our source and to be separated from our God. The devil will use distractions and hindrances, and will pull out his arsenal of weapons to cause you to lose focus. He will try to make you look to the left or to the right for other sources. But remember, he is already defeated because the battle belongs to the Lord.

We must understand why it is necessary for adversities to come in our lives. As followers of Jesus, we must become Over comers. And as we overcome adversities like hardships, misfortunes, afflictions; they no longer have control over us because the lesson is more valuable than the pain! The word declares that God delivers us out of them all.

There will be wilderness time where we wander. But the amount of time we wander will be determined by how we view our trails, our afflictions, our misfortunes, our sorrow, and our oppressions. The great lie Satan wants you to believe is, that as sold out Christians, these adversities just should not happen, they should pass over us. This is a direct contradiction to what God's word says.

Everyone knows adversities will come from time to time. They just invite themselves without us doing a thing. However, how we host adversities will make a world of difference in their outcome. For example: when we choose to walk in disappointment, when we hold on to unforgiveness of others including ourselves, or when we entertain and allow the adversity to be greater than our God, these will affect the outcome. It all boils down to how you choose to handle the adversity. It can cripple you or release you.

Firstly; adversities will come in disguises, making us think we are the only one going through such hardship, sickness, financial calamity, marriage trouble. Secondly; how we respond to them will be urgently important in these last days. And thirdly; we cannot get caught up with the drama of the circumstances and lose focus of the bigger picture thus surrendering our authority to the adversity itself.

It's ironic that our adversity can help us find strength through the Holy Spirit who is your friend, teacher, guide, comforter and most importantly, the Spirit of Truth. One of my favorite scripture says: *"If you faint in the day of adversity, your strength is small" (Proverb 24:10).* I am grateful for the lessons I've learned. Had I not gone through the malpractice trial, the loss of retirement money, the mission trip to India, and the battle with depression, I would not have known that our God gives power to the weak, and to those that have no might, He increases our strength. Many of you are facing adversities right now during these very difficult times. There's a whole lot of shaking going on all over the world.

And, the Spirit of Truth is revealing to those who put their trust in the matchless name of Jesus that they should not faint. We serve a God who is neither weary nor does He faint, so hold on and finish strong. As Isaiah states: *"those who wait on the Lord shall renew their strength, they shall mount up with wings like eagles, they shall run and not be weary, and they shall walk and not faint."*

VOICE Magazine had an article by Apostle Jonas Clark that discussed 'Eight Steps' in which to overcome adversity. When people have gone around the mountain enough times like I have, they learn revelation truths. Many of the responses previously shared are reflective of the eight steps discussed in this article. Let me share Apostle Jonas' eight steps to overcoming adversity coupled with some revelations of my own.

Eight Steps to Overcoming Adversity

1. Run to Jesus

When adversity attacks, the first thing you should do is run to Jesus. Don't flake out, shut down, break rank or isolate yourself from those who can help you. Run to Jesus; remember that Jesus is the author and finisher of your faith. He said, *"I will never leave you nor forsake you." (Hebrews 13:5)* After you run to Jesus check your heart. Go down your personal checklist and examine yourself. Ask Him to search your heart too, sometimes there are hidden and camouflaged transgressions. And if you have violated the Word in anyway, repent. Running to Jesus coupled with repentance should always be your first reaction to adversity.

2. Cast All Your Cares

The next weapon in our arsenal against adversity is casting all our cares on Jesus. The Scriptures tell us, *"Cast all your cares on Him for He cares for you."* *(I Peter 5:7)* Repeat this as many times as necessary until your adversary knows who you are and in whom you serve and trust. That's what casting means; TRUST. Satan will not leave you alone until you do so.

3. Encourage Yourself

Encouragement is another powerful antidote against adversity. When we stop putting the Word in our hearts, that's when we put our lives in jeopardy. With the Word of God written solidly on the tablets of your heart you can encourage yourself as David did. The Psalms are full of David's prayers of deliverance from oppressors. One of David's greatest characteristics was that he never gave up, he refused to quit. So it should be the same with us.

4. Submit and Resist

Freedom from adversity will come when you draw near to God. His Word declares He will draw near to you. In His presence, any contradictions to His ways will bring convic-

tion. Don't be surprised. Instead, submit and receive the forgiveness you need and then you can move to the next part.
Say to your adversary 'it is written', just as Jesus did when
He resisted the same temptations that are in the world; the
lust of the flesh, the pride of life, and the lust of the eyes.
*"Therefore submit to God. Resist the devil and he will flee
from thee." (James 4:7)*

5. Speak in Your Situation

Speak to your situation. Tell the adversary that it is
written that no weapon formed against you shall prosper.
That God is your only source and you're totally reliant upon
Him. Look not to the left nor the right. It is He that estab-
lishes you as you commit your ways to Him. Remember to
thank Jesus that it's His strength and His face (His Presence)
you seek, forever. Go find scripture that applies to your situation and hold fast to it and do this until your adversary
stands in awe of your God.

6. Let Faith Fight for You

Let hope arise in you right now. You are already standing
in victory. Our faith is one of our most powerful weapons we
have. The Armor of God has a shield of faith that quenches

every fiery dart your adversary will throw at you. These fiery darts can be distractions, hindrances and decoys in order to get you to relinquish your authority. The Shield of faith is your trust in the accomplished work of Jesus. He is victorious because He accomplished all that His father gave Him to do. And He now awaits His full inheritance...us! We also await our inheritance, eternity. Jesus overcame the world and was victorious and we will too, by the blood of the Lamb. (I John 5:4) Rejoice in the faith you have in Christ. Endure hardship like a good soldier and put your armor in place as a warrior for Christ. This will assure you the victory.

7. Pray in Tongues

Speaking in tongues allows the Holy Spirit to pray and strengthen you when you pray in the Spirit. This is important, vital and essential since Spirit speaks to spirit and the Spirit is directly talking to God for you. He will help you to pray when you do not know what you ought to pray. If you want your prayers to be strengthened, start reading the Word, meditating on scripture, and allowing the Holy Spirit to pray through you and make sure to ask and inquire for understanding. *"If I pray in an unknown tongue my spirit prayeth." (I Corinthians 14:14)* Remember, speaking in tongues is one of the many gifts God gives His children, all you need to do is ask.

8. Get Back to Church

It's very important to listen when God gives specific instruction. An example of this is Hebrews 10:25 when God says; " *Not forsaking the assembling of ourselves together as is the manner of some, but exhorting one another, and so much the more as you see the day approaching.*" Seek God as to where you are to be, then come alongside the visionary and partner where God has placed you. It is God's perfect design that we need other Christians to understand fully His perfect love for us.

Adversity attacks everybody, but how you handle it fulfills *'thy kingdom come thy will be done on earth as it is in heaven'*. It is your response to adversity that helps others to receive the kingdom of God at hand. Romans 8:28 tells us; *"And we know that all things will work together for good to those whom love him and are called according to His purpose."*

It is time for the Bride of Christ to know that God loves them and that He has a purpose for each one of us. That purpose is to do what He created you to do, to bring Him pleasure. You should not try to be better than the next guy, or envious of the call on another one's life. Your obedience to His will pleases Him. I Corinthian 12:18 tell us...."*But now God has set members each one of them in the body just as He pleased.*" And that we all fit together doing our part with our whole heart. When Jesus was asked what was 'the greatest commandment in the law', His answer was; "*Thou shalt love the LORD thy God with all thy heart, and with all thy soul, with all thy mind. This is the first and greatest commandment. And the second is like unto it. Thou shalt love thy neighbor as thyself. On these two commandments hang all the law and the prophets.*" *(Matthew 22:37-40)*

God is still speaking through his prophets. The only way a false prophet enters into the fold is through deceit and by imitating a true prophet. Our God is still manifesting His presence today, just like He did with the children of Israel. He uses fire, clouds, angels and burning bushes. Let me tell you, during the vision, I experienced and witnessed God's manifested presence just as the children of Israel did when they wandered through the desert. God's presence came in the form of a thick cloud that filled the temple and bellowed over our heads. And everyone under His manifested presence that was sick was healed and demons began to cry out. Sickness cannot remain in God's presence and the demons will have no choice but to speak out and to cry out.

What will it take for the billions of lost souls to seek, call, search and pray to God? Yes that's right, the manifested glory of God, accompanied by miracles, signs and wonders. As many as were needed, were saved and added to the church daily.

When the church was birthed in the book of Acts, these believers diligently assembled themselves in unity, acted in one accord and prayed awaiting for the promise of God. As a result, they were filled with the manifested presence of God. This still applies to believers today. God has promised to empower us to be His witnesses, in Jerusalem, Judea, Samaria and the uttermost parts of the earth.

The glory will be manifested in those that have been through the fire just like the Hebrew boys, and Daniel in the lion's den. They did not bow down or serve any other gods. And like Stephen, as he looked up and saw Jesus on the right hand of God and commended his spirit to God, he overcame adversity. And Peter, walking out his guilt and condemnation of denying Christ three times, later preaching Jesus glorified. Hallelujah!

O God of the Host, with many angels at your beaconing call, help us to recognize you are still manifesting your glorious presence in this hour. Just like the days of old, O' Ancient of Days when Elijah was caught up with wings of chariots, John on the Isle of Patmos, Enoch was no more and Paul called up to the third heavens. IT IS TIME for all that believe to progress towards the Glorious Bride as complete and mature Christians, having no blemish or wrinkle. I can't express this enough, IT IS TIME!

And it is my prayer that I continuously pray for the body of Christ, just as Paul prayed for the Ephesians: *"Therefore I also, after I heard of your faith in the Lord Jesus and your love for all saints, do not cease to give thanks for you in my prayers: that the God of our Lord Jesus Christ, the Father of glory, may give to you the spirit of wisdom and revelation in the knowledge of Him, the eyes of your understanding being enlightened; that you may know what is the hope of His calling, what are the riches of the glory of His inheritance in the saints, and what is the exceeding greatness of His power toward us who believe according to the working of His mighty power which He worked in Christ when he raised Him from the dead and seated Him at His right hand in the heavenly places, far above all principality and power and might that is named, not only in this age but also in that which is to come. And He put all things under his feet, and gave Him to be head over all things to the church, which is His body, the fullness of Him who fills all in all." (Ephesians 2:15-23)*

When the enemy senses God's presence resting on your life you can correctly suspect there will inevitably be envy, jealousy and strife because of your success. At the time David was serving Saul, he was devoted, loyal and forgiving, in spite of the many things Saul did to destroy David's popularity and success. Saul even ordered his son Jonathan and his servant to kill David. But, like David in Psalms 35 and 109, we can ask God to execute judgment to those who are trying to harm or destroy us.

Whether the attack is on your ministry or on your personal life, you will find that God is more than able to protect you like he did David. It is wise for you to seek counsel of mature men and women of faith. Leave out the drama and the circumstances and focus on allowing others to help you walk out your faith through the difficult periods in your life. David had Jonathan and Michal; Saul's son and daughter, to help him escape. But even more important, David sought out wise counsel.

After David was anointed King, his first recorded success was to capture the city of Jerusalem, even after being told that it was impossible. (2 Sam 5:5-9) The capture of Jerusalem had nothing to do with David's wisdom or his military intuition. It was because the God of hosts was with him. And the reason for David's continuing success was because he honored God. Unlike most of us, David was quick to recognize and repent for his mistakes, weaknesses and faults, and he consistently gave God all the glory.

It was during my difficult times that repentance became first nature to me, even when I thought I wasn't wrong. An example of this is when I asked God to forgive me for electing to have the Gastric-bypass surgery. I had altered what God had fearfully and wonderfully made. Sometimes it is so easy to blame others. Forgiving this doctor was not something that came easy for me especially since it caused me so much pain. And the lesson I learn from it all is that God is to be glorified even in our suffering, pain, and grief. We primarily learn and gain wisdom and restoration when we look inside, instead of blaming others on the outside.

Always make sure your personal life and your ministry line up together. David led by example, both as a spiritual leader and as a military leader. He trusted in God's timing and purpose rather than to take matters into his own hands. It is when we are abiding in God's presence that we become true worshipers of God. When David abided and trusted, he was able to inquire of God as I did when I was called to India. And most importantly, when success came, he gave God the glory.

"And it came to pass after this that David inquired of the LORD, saying, Shall I go up into any of the cities of Judah? And the LORD said unto him, Go up. And David said, Whither shall I go up? And he said, Unto Hebron. So David went up thither... Then the people of Judah came to Hebron and anointed David to be king over the tribe of Judah." (2 Samuel 2: 1-4)

It took years for God to perfect, teach and prepare David so that his personal life lined up with his purpose. David's first anointing by Samuel was at the age of 15, and his second anointing, as Judah's king was at the age of thirty. Throughout David's reign, we can see the evidence of God's Presence as He works to bring about His will at His due season. God sees the big picture, the whole picture.

I have found myself like David as he was trying to bring the Ark of the Covenant back to Jerusalem so that it would be closer to him. In his disregard, David transported it back in an ox cart. This was not the proper way to transport the Ark of God, so when the oxen stumbled and Uzzah, one of the soldiers reached out to protect the Ark, he was struck dead. David was so grieved. David's disrespectful choices resulted in the death of a fellow Israelite and the Ark of the Covenant was left behind in the care of a Levite name ObedEdom.

The ObedEdom household was being blessed because the Ark was in their care. They knew the importance in respectfully handling of the things of God, and of what the Ark represented to His chosen people. Through this experience David learned a vital lesson and the importance of the proper honor and handling of God's presence.

I also have recognized that I was allowing the way I responded to attacks to affect the handling of God's presence in my own life. And like David, it took me a while to learn the proper handling so that I may please God. I'm not afraid to admit to God, "I'm wrong, please help me do it your way".

David did return to bring the ark back to Jerusalem, but this time he took special care to do it God's way. This time the Levites carried the ark, sacrifices were made and offered every six steps as respect and acknowledgement to God's ways they honored His presence. I have learned to guard the presence of God at all cost; by being diligent to God's ways not mine, and to study the word of God in order to understand His character and His ways. And when I mess up, I quickly ask for God's forgiveness and ask Him to; *"teach me your ways, please don't allow my ways to cause your presence to be taken from me" (Psalm 51: 10).*

I can't leave you until I share with you what you are to do when you are faced with persecution and attacks that are all geared to leave you void of the precious presence of the Lord; Your Savior, your Redeemer, and the Restorer of your life.

The following Scriptures are God's instructions for believers, in how we are to properly handle His presence when attacks and persecution come

How to Handle Attacks and Persecution

1. MEDITATE ON THE WORD OF GOD

   (Psalm 7:1) *"O Lord in you I put my trust. Save me from all those who persecute me and deliver me."* This particular Psalm is a meditation of David's, which he sang to the LORD concerning his flight from Saul and his men the Benjamites.

2. REJOICE

(Matthew 5:12) "Rejoice and be exceedingly glad for great is your reward in heaven, for so they persecuted the prophets who were before you." Not only rejoice but also count yourself worthy to suffer for the cause of Christ. Be exceedingly glad, radically rejoicing when you feel like crying, when you feel like you can't go on. Rejoice, again I say rejoice.

3. LOVE

(Matthew 5:44) "But I say to you love your enemies, Bless those who curse you, do good to those who hate you and pray for those who spitefully use you and persecute you." It is not just a matter of sentiment alone but practical concern, blessing, praying and positive wishes for well-being. These are extended to friends and enemies alike. It's hard to hate someone that you are praying for.

4. ENDURE

(I CORINTHIANS 4:12) *"And we labor, working with our own hands, being reviled, we bless, being persecuted we endure."* Enduring means not losing courage under pressure, persevering, tolerating, bearing with, putting up with, standing firm. It's God's strong right hand that's enabling you to endure and he will hold you up with it. *(Isaiah 41:10)* *"I will help you, I will uphold you with my victorious right hand."*

5. GLORIFY GOD AND GLORIFY JESUS

(I Peter 4:16) *"Yet if anyone suffers as a Christian, let him not be ashamed but let him glorify God in this matter."* This is one of three times the word Christian appears in the New Testament. The other two are in (Acts 11:26; 26:23). Peter also said, *"if you are reproached for the name of Jesus, blessed are you, for the Spirit of glory and of God rest upon you. On their part He is blasphemed, but on your part He is glorified."* (I Peter 4:14)

6. COMMIT YOUR SOUL

(I Peter 4:19) *"Therefore let those who suffer according to the will of God commit their souls to Him in doing good, as to a faithful Creator."* I tell you in these last

days it's important to devote yourself to loving Jesus, even when you can't see Him amidst the suffering and the pain. Love Him by believing every one of His promises by faith. Allow joy unspeakable, full of glory, to rest upon you even in your suffering. Remember Stephen in the book of Acts when he was being stoned. The glory shined all about him and he was able to look up and see Jesus at the right hand of the Father, and he asked the Father to commit his spirit and to forgive those who were stoning him. Like our Messiah, after being beaten mercilessly and enduring the death of the cross, Jesus said to the Father, *"into your hands I commit my spirit,"* and then said *"it was finished."*

Yes, I can attest to many of the characters in the Bible, however, I seem to relate and parallel David's life more than anyone else's. David was humble but not without mistakes. He demonstrated that he loved God with all his heart, mind and strength. Yes, I can identify with David like his rise to leadership over Judah. This captivates the big picture I spoke of earlier that God knows. God's purpose is revealed all the way through to the book of Revelation. There is a parallel between the reign of David over Judah and the magnificent power and character of our resurrected LORD and soon coming King.

I know that God's blessings are by His grace and grace alone. He paid the price, paid in full. And if He could use David, as imperfect as he was, He can use me, even you! My life is a daily effort to try to live with a heart like David's. I always try to joyfully meditate on the word of God, to rejoice, to love, to bless and to endure. In everything I do, I give glory to Him and His Son, Jesus, who overcame so that He may be glorified in me.

"And I saw in the right hand of Him who sat on the throne, a scroll written inside and on the back, sealed with seven seals. Then I saw a strong angel proclaiming with a loud voice, "who is worthy to open the scroll and to loose its seal?" And no one in heaven or on the earth or under the earth was able to open the scroll, or to look at it. So I wept much, because no one was found worthy to open and read the scroll, or to look at it. But one of the elders said to me. "Do not weep. Behold the Lion of the tribe of Judah, the Root of David, has prevailed to open the scroll to loose it's seven seals." (Revelation 5:1-5)

The heavens are searching for people who are worthy to inaugurate God's dramatic conclusion to world history. Judgment has begun, dear Body of Christ. Who do you want to pattern your life after? Is it the one who has triumphed, the same one who created everything, including you? The one who created all of us for His pleasure?

Through this book I've tried to share my soul, heart and my intellect with you to let you know that the things God had shown me twenty years ago is real and we all need to be ready for Jesus' return. Be Watchful! Please believe me, when I say there is a judgment seat for believers, I witnessed it. Every little detail of your life will be brought up and judged. Your motives, your conduct, your disposition, your posture, your character, your displays of anger, your jealousies and mistrusts, they all will be brought before you like a digital picture frame, one segment at a time. That which will keep will not burn.

Start from this moment on, living in light of eternity! Be a true Christian in every sense of the word, a follower of Jesus. Only when we are abiding in God's presence, can we become true worshipers of God.

Follow hard after Him by seeking to obey Him with your whole heart. Determine in your heart to obey His word.

Finish strong, work while it is day, and keep looking up for our redemption draws near. I encourage you and build you up in the holy faith, in love, and I admonish you to let nothing cause you to be without His Presence, now and eternally.

Scripture Index

Foreword

Preface

His Presence Guides Us

His Presence Teaches Us

His Presence Leads Us

His Presence Comforts Us

Abiding in His Presence

ABOUT THE AUTHOR

Carolyn Ruth Washington, a retired Physical Education, Health teacher and coach, lives in Miami, Florida with her daughter and 'triplet' granddaughters. Rev. Washington is a credentialed minister with the 'Assemblies of God'. She has served tirelessly as a Bible Study teacher, intercessor and Sunday school teacher for many years.

Since her early years as a believer, Carolyn has been a dedicated student of theology. With a consuming passion, she has been on a mission to deploy God's love through biblical knowledge, wisdom and understanding.

She also serves as Spiritual Advisor with 'Kairos Prison Ministry', a bible study teacher with 'Woman's Agape'; a residential treatment center, and heads up the intercessory prayer team for women's conferences.

Her heart is with intercession and restoration. As the founder and President of CRW Ministries, Inc. (Captives Restoration Warriors), God has called her to help equip 'the captives' into the awareness of who they are in Him and restore them to become what they are purposed and destined to do; Developing Kingdom Warriors!

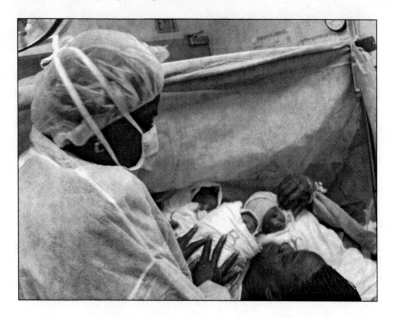

You can find

Carolyn Ruth Washington

and

CRW Ministries' online at:

www.crwministries.org

CPSIA information can be obtained at www.ICGtesting.com
Printed in the USA
LVOW120927080112

262776LV00001B/3/P